Poverty
in Canada

RAGHUBAR D. SHARMA

ISSUES IN CANADA

OXFORD
UNIVERSITY PRESS

OXFORD
UNIVERSITY PRESS

Oxford University Press is a department of the University of Oxford.
It furthers the University's objec tive of excellence in research, scholarship,
and education by publishing worldwide. Oxford is a registered trade mark of
Oxford University Press in the UK and in certain other countries.

Published in Canada by
Oxford University Press
8 Sampson Mews, Suite 204,
Don Mills, Ontario M3C 0H5 Canada

www.oupcanada.com

Library and Archives Canada Cataloguing in Publication

Sharma, Raghubar D., 1947–
Poverty in Canada / Raghubar Sharma.

(Issues in Canada)
Includes bibliographical references and index.
ISBN 978-0-19-900322-8

1. Poverty—Canada. 2. Poor—Canada. 3. Canada—
Economic conditions—1991–. I. Title. II. Series: Issues in
Canada

HC120.P6S53 2012   362.50971   C2012-902402-3

Cover image: Copyright luxorphoto, 2012
Used under license from Shutterstock.com

Printed and bound in the United States of America

1 2 3 4 — 15 14 13 12

To my parents;
my brothers, Kewal and Kamal;
Rudolf K. Kogler, a pioneer Ontario demographer;
and Mr. Richard Schmidt, president of Liquid Carbonics Canada,
my first employer in Canada

In loving memory of my brother
Salig Ram Sharma (1926–2011)

Contents

List of Illustrations

Acknowledgements

I would like to thank Lorne Tepperman for considering this book for the Issues in Canada series. Several people at Oxford University Press are responsible for bringing this project to fruition. I am thankful to Kristina Koitsopoulos and Mark Thomas for bringing my proposal to the attention of my editor Jennie Rubio. Many thanks to Jennie for her help in restructuring the manuscript and suggesting new ideas, issues, and arguments. Her many hours of hard work is highly appreciated. I am also thankful to Katie Scott for her help in bringing the book to its final form. Finally, I want to express my gratitude to my brother Jagdish S. Sharma whose Air France ticket made my Canadian journey possible.

Introduction

The first time I taught a course on the sociology of poverty was in the mid-1970s at the University of Alberta. Since then, I have taken a keen interest in this social problem. There was no consensus on a single definition of poverty in Canada at that time, and there is no such consensus even today. One of the reasons for the lack of consensus is that the experience of poverty for each individual is unique—poverty is as diverse as human beings are. At the same time, sociologists have not been able to put poverty into any broad theoretical framework, though there have been several attempts at the conceptualization of poverty since the 1960s. In view of this lack of consensus, this book explores the literature on poverty in Canada to enable the reader to make his or her own judgment.

Since the all-party resolution of Parliament on child poverty in 1989, the main focus of attention in Canada has been child poverty. But this ignores the fact that poor children do not face poverty in isolation; they live in families with parents and grandparents, and belong to the diverse ethnic mosaic of Canada. The second purpose of this book, then, is to take a holistic approach, that is, to include all the major disadvantaged demographic groups in the discussion.

As a result of improved communications technology and the impetus to simplify trade barriers between nations, companies are moving across international borders. While the consequences of this globalization for Canada's poor cannot be fully discussed in a short book on poverty, I feel that it is important to help readers understand the impact of this massive transformation. The third purpose of this book, therefore, will be to highlight some links between globalization, increased inequality, and the present-day conflicts and protests.

How poverty is defined and measured in Canada is provided in the appendix. Understanding numbers and rates is one thing, but of course understanding poverty as a concept is a different matter altogether. Chapter 1 will examine how poverty is understood as a concept. The next five chapters will focus on poverty among disadvantaged demographic groups in Canada: ethnic groups, the elderly, women, children, and workers. Chapter 7 will examine regional poverty in Canada. Chapter 8 will attempt to understand the phenomenon of reverse movement of global wealth due to globalization and its implications in terms of increasing social inequality, which lies at the centre of the social unrest manifesting in such protests as the 2011 Occupy movements and the Arab Spring. The chapter will conclude with an assessment of Canada's place in the global economy in 2050.

This may be one of the first concise books on poverty in Canada that is intended for general readers as well as for students, teachers, policy makers, sociologists, economists, and social workers interested in the area of poverty and inequality.

A book that surveys a wide range of literature has to consult a wide range of resources. Due care has been taken to credit the sources used in the book. Any omission in referencing is, of course, unintentional and, once pointed out, will be rectified in the next edition.

Chapter 1

Understanding Poverty

Introduction

Social inequality is universal. It is an important aspect of every society. Individuals have different attributes, occupy different statuses in the social structure, and play different occupational roles in the society. These roles are rewarded differentially in terms of money, status, and prestige. Almost every society is stratified into various social and economic classes on the basis of a differential reward system. This system is called social stratification. The study of stratification is the study of classes in the society. Poverty is a condition associated with the lower class, but poverty is also studied with concepts that are independent of concepts of stratification. The major sociological concepts that are helpful to understanding poverty are the culture of poverty, the situational perspective, the stigma of poverty, and social exclusion.

The Culture of Poverty

The culture of poverty sees poverty as a subculture, with its own values and normative system. In sociology and anthropology, *subculture* is a term used for a cultural group whose values and norms are different but are not in direct contradiction with the values and norms of the larger culture in which the subculture exists. The term is frequently used with respect to youth and minority groups. There is a distinction between a subculture and a contraculture (also termed *counterculture*). The contraculture is a cultural group whose values and norms are in contradiction with those of the larger culture—for example, the delinquent gang subculture (Yinger 1960). Paradoxically, sociologists have implied both subculture and contraculture concepts in their discussion of poverty as a culture.

Lewis (1966) formulated the concept of the culture of poverty based on his studies of poverty in the United States, Mexico, and Puerto Rico. He observed that the victims of poverty exhibit distinct actions, spending habits, and values in slums that form a distinct culture that can be called the culture of poverty. He listed 70 characteristics of the culture of poverty to make his point, including the following: a low level of organization, overcrowding, gregariousness, unprotected childhood, early initiation to sex, female-headed households, mother-centred families, and little privacy. Finally, he argued that the concept of the culture of poverty might correct some misunderstandings regarding the characteristics of poverty. For example, some sociologists consider the high incidence of consensual unions among poor African-Americans one of the historical consequences of slavery. These sociologists contend that the African-American community of the United States was unable to develop a stable family system because of frequent displacement imposed upon them by the practice of slavery. Common-law arrangements and "desertion" become an alternative for marriage and divorce for the poor who are unable to afford the legal and financial difficulties of marriage and divorce.

If poverty is a culture, how does this culture develop? According to culturalists, society fails to provide social, political, and economic organization to low-income populations. The poor do not participate in such middle-class institutions as social clubs, universities, and banks. This disengagement from middle-class institutions alienates the poor from mainstream society, and as a result, the poor develop alternative institutions, such as the consensual unions noted above. These alternative institutions are perpetuated over generations. Lewis (1966) asserts that a slum child learns the values of the culture of poverty by the age of seven and after that he or she is unable to adjust to the values of the larger society. Fatalism, a fear of authority, and suspicion of the institutions of the majority society are some of the characteristics of the outcome of the isolation of the poor from mainstream society.

At the same time, the poor are aware of the values of the middle class and claim them as their own. But in the face of a lack of a steady job and adequate income, they are unable to afford these values. For example, they believe in the institution of marriage as outlined by the middle-class norms, but in the absence of a steady job and adequate income, common-law arrangements make more sense. Similarly, desertion—a value frowned upon by the middle class—becomes a poor person's divorce in the face of financial difficulties.

Lewis (1966) agrees that not all poor form a culture of poverty. There are poor populations with a high degree of social organization. The low-caste destitute of India were always integrated in the occupational structure of the caste system, and they even had their own self-governing body, called

Panchayat. Jews of Eastern Europe who lived in poverty had a tradition of literacy and a cohesive social organization. According to Lewis (1966), the most likely candidates for the culture of poverty are the lower strata of rapidly developing societies. The culture of poverty is endemic to the free enterprise, pre-welfare stage of capitalism. It is also endemic to the colonized in colonial societies in which native culture has been disrupted by the colonizer, for example, the Aboriginal peoples of North America. Lewis (1966) believes that some 20 percent of the poor live in the culture of poverty in the United States. They include African-Americans, Puerto Ricans, Mexicans, American Indians, and the southern poor whites.

The concept of the culture of poverty can be illustrated with four social indicators: crime, mental illness, education, and family life.

Crime

Miller (1958) was the first to argue that lower-class gang delinquency is a direct product of lower-class culture. He believes that patterns of focal concerns are significantly different in the lower class than in the middle class. *Focal concern* is a term used for such social psychological traits as trouble, toughness, smartness, excitement, fate, and autonomy. Miller (1958) believes that these traits are defined differently in the lower class than in the middle class. For example, in a delinquent subculture, smartness is defined not in terms of scholastic ability but as a capacity to outsmart, outfox, and con. Miller (1958) therefore believes that gang delinquency is not a violation of middle-class norms but rather a product of the lower-class culture that has unique focal concerns conducive to unique patterns of behaviour.

Mental illness

Studies show an inverse correlation between mental illness (schizophrenia) and socio-economic class (Hudson 2005). There are two views of poverty-related schizophrenia, both of which are grounded in the cultural perspective. Banfield (1970) believes that lower-class culture is different from the middle-class culture and that it is pathological. The high incidence of schizophrenia is a testimony to this pathology. Sutherland (1949), on the other hand, says that the correlation between social class and schizophrenia is a product of biased labelling. Most psychiatrists come from the middle class, so because of their class expectations of "normal" behaviour they are more likely to label certain lower-class behaviour as mental illness. Psychiatrists' own class-bound values lead them to label perfectly "normal" lower-class behaviour as indicative of mental illness that has arisen from a unique culture of poverty.

Education

Davis (1948) points out that a lower-class child is faced with insecurities that are unknown to a middle-class child. For example, in an environment in which the food supply is insecure, children develop "food anxiety." Similarly, they also develop anxiety of eviction, of too little sleep, and of being cold in winter. A poor child's anxieties regarding education also differ from those of a middle-class child. Middle-class children learn to fear poor grades, being aggressive toward the teacher, fighting, and having early sexual relations. By contrast, poor children who belong to a delinquent gang learn quite opposite fears from their gang members. They fear being labelled a "softie" with the teacher. Peer pressure leads to homework completion being viewed as a kind of disgrace, and good grades may be concealed from their peers. Originally, Davis (1948) pointed out that these goals—which may appear odd to those from the middle class—make sense in the context of impoverished surroundings. In other words, the source of problems of lower-class children in school can be traced to their socialization and culture.

Family life

There is a clear relationship between social class and family size. In most societies, lower-class families have higher birth rates and a greater number of children compared to middle- or upper-class families. Culturalists would assert that the poor have too many babies as a result of their cultural beliefs. There is an inverse relationship between family size and income in developed societies. Research published in the 1970s (Balakrishnan, Kantner, and Allingham 1975) showed that in Canada, family size and income showed a U-shaped relationship. In other words, upper- and lower-income families had more children than did middle-income families.

The Situational Perspective

The situational perspective (also called the structural perspective) sees the traits of the culture of poverty as a reaction to surrounding conditions (termed *environment*). In this perspective, a unique culture does not lead to different behaviour; on the contrary, the poor believe in the values of the middle class but lack the means to realize them. Situationalists argue that the solution is not for the poor to alter their culture but rather for their surroundings to change to help them escape poverty.

The same four variables—crime, mental illness, education, and family life—that were demonstrated above for the culture of poverty can be used to explain the situational perspective.

Crime

One of the most persuasive explanations of the relationship between poverty and crime is still Merton's 1938 article on social structure and anomie (which means a lack of the usual social or ethical standards). He observed that there are areas in southeastern Europe that have lower crime rates in spite of higher poverty rates. There must be something different about poverty in the United States and its high correlation with crime. Merton (1938) believes that the norms of the American culture place an emphasis on economic success. For a middle-class American, economic success is a cultural goal, and education is a prescribed institutional norm or a means to attain this goal. Merton (1938) asserts that the poor believe in the middle-class goal of economic success but that the prescribed means—in this case, the education—to attain this goal are not available to them. This creates a state of normlessness, or anomie, among the poor. As result of this state of anomie, lacking the middle-class means (i.e., education), the poor take up an alternative means (i.e., crime) to obtain the same middle-class goal of being an economic success through making money.

Sociologists who try to explain crime with the help of Merton's theory of anomie believe that lower-class crime takes place as a result of structural constraints faced by the poor. They believe that delinquent gangs develop under some particular social and geographical conditions. Park and Burgess (1925) in their pioneer ecological analysis suggested that urban growth takes place in concentric zones. The first, central concentric zone in an urban area is the central business district. The second, "transition" zone, is the zone into which and out of which residents may move frequently. Characterized by transients, this zone is highly prone to delinquency and conditions of poverty. The working class lives in the third zone. The fourth zone consists of a suburban population who can afford individual transportation. Urban poverty in this sense is an outcome of the nature of the growth of cities.

Mental illness

According to the situational or structural school, the higher rates of schizophrenia in the lower class are a result of the lower-class environment. A study conducted in Maryland in the United States (Clausen and Kohn 1959) found no correlation between social class and schizophrenia per se. This research did reveal, however, that the size of the city is an important predictor of schizophrenia. In smaller towns, where there is integration between the social classes, there is no correlation. But in larger cities there is an inverse correlation between social class and schizophrenia due to the lack of social integration. Freedman (1975) showed that the density intensifies the effects of negative conditions already existing in a lower-class milieu. The Canadian psychiatrist Abram Hoffer (1962) reported success in treating certain forms of schizophrenia with injections of the vitamin niacin. He argued that the lower class is most likely to suffer from vitamin deficiency, especially niacin deficiency and that this deficiency may trigger schizophrenia. Dunham (1965) offers another explanation in the form of what is known as drift hypothesis. According to this hypothesis, it is not the poverty that causes schizophrenia; it is the schizophrenia that causes individuals to drift into poverty.

These explanations of the relationship between poverty and schizophrenia are situational in nature. They hold that under certain situations, be it density or niacin deficiency, a relationship between poverty and schizophrenia manifests.

Education

According to culturalists, the causes of the high school dropout rates and the difficulties with school faced by lower-class children can be traced to socialization. According to situationalists, the inadequacies in the school system and the negative attitude of the education system toward lower-class children are responsible for the higher dropout rates and increased learning difficulties faced by poor children. According to Clark (1967), lower-class children face learning difficulties because of ineffective teaching and teachers' belief that the poor cannot learn. Where culturalists would emphasize culture enrichment programs for lower-class children, situationalists would argue that changing teachers' training and attitudes, as well as curricula and textbooks, can ameliorate the difficulties faced in education by children in poverty.

Family life

In the situational perspective, the poor have too many babies not because of their cultural values but because of their structural conditions, which limit their access to birth control and knowledge of family planning (Jaffe and Polgar 1968). In many societies, poor women desire a smaller family size but end up having more children than they wanted due to lack of accessibility to birth control (Sharma 1980).

This notion is backed up by research from India (Roche 1976). After 25 years of experience with the government policy of family planning, an Indian government spokesperson participating in the Bucharest

Conference on Population concluded that high birth rates are caused by poverty and that integrating economic development programs with family welfare programs is needed to reverse the trend. As India started developing economically, its fertility started declining. According to this argument, high fertility is not so much a lower-class value as it is a consequence of the conditions of poverty—which are conducive to high fertility.

Stigma of Poverty

Some sociologists who were critical of the cultural perspective provided the situational perspective as an alternative. Still others thought that both perspectives took extreme positions. Waxman (1977) is an example of a researcher who takes a different approach again, arguing that we must understand the nature of the relationship between the poor and the non-poor in order to be able to develop a perspective on poverty. He used Goffman's (1963a) work on the sociology of stigma to develop a new framework, which was later termed *the stigma of poverty*.

Development of the stigma of poverty

Human beings evaluate other humans being with respect to the attributes they possess. Stigma refers to a particular kind of negative social perception of certain human attributes. Goffman (1963b) describes three types of stigma:

1. Physical stigma: social perception of such attributes as physical defects or deformities.
2. Tribal stigma: social perception of such attributes as race, nationality, and religion.
3. Blemishes of individual characters: social perception of such attributes as a known record of imprisonment, addiction, alcoholism, mental disorder, homosexuality, and unemployment.

All types of stigma interfere with normal interaction (Goffman 1963b). The belief that poverty is a lack of effort stigmatizes the poor and interferes in the interaction between the poor and the non-poor; even the welfare system, which is designed to help the poor, helps the process of stigmatization by isolating the poor (Waxman 1977). As a response to stigma, the poor develop certain traits, which may look like a culture.

Waxman (1977) declares that although he examines poverty as a group stigma, his analysis is not meant to blame the poor. Nor is it meant to apply to all the poor.

Responses to the stigma of poverty

Goffman (1963b) believes that there are three possible strategies that stigmatized persons may follow to avoid interaction with "normal" persons. First, they may associate with those who possess the same stigma or associate with only those "normal" persons who are sympathetic toward their stigma. Second, they may try to hide their identity from "normal" persons. Third, they may act on the meanings that "normal" persons give them. In all these three possibilities, there is a common factor; that is, the stigmatized person tries to adjust to stigma. Similarly, once a group is stigmatized, it may also develop certain techniques to adjust to the group stigma. The stigma of poverty is likely to result in a cluster of traits that are used by the poor to adjust to the stigma, and these traits have been described by culturalists as the culture of poverty (Waxman 1977).

Mead (1934) believes that the self has two aspects. The aspect of the self that develops through interaction with others is called "me." The other aspect of the self remains the individual's own identity; this aspect of the self is called "I." Waxman (1977) believes that because of the stigma of poverty, the poor remain culturally isolated and their "me" is quite different from that of the non-poor. In other words, the poor do not fully internalize the values and the norms of society, though they are aware of them.

Waxman (1977) contends that the situationalists are wrong in saying that the poor adhere to society's values, and that the culturalists are wrong in saying that the poor have an alternative culture. According to Waxman (1977), as a result of stigmatization and isolation of the poor, there is a somewhat less than successful internalization of any culture; a poor person's real "me" is an existential "me"; he or she is not making, but getting by. Waxman (1977) argues that the higher crime rate in the lower class is a survival technique. In school also, a poor child is just biding time until he or she can drop out because the stigma manifests itself more prominently in school than in the community. Waxman (1977) believes that adjustments to the stigma of poverty are transmitted intergenerationally through socialization, and he emphasizes that the persistence of poverty and the behaviour of the poor cannot be attributed solely to cultural and situational sources. In other words, poverty persists as long as stigma persists.

Social Exclusion

Anglo-Saxon liberal tradition looked at poverty as a natural condition, governed by the laws of population and resources. Malthus's theory (1826) is couched in this tradition. Many researchers believe that the nature of poverty and the perception of poverty have changed to such an extent that a new term is needed (Rodgers, Gore, and Figueiredo 1995; Room 1995; Paugam 1996; Jordan 1996; Alcock 1993). The continental European tradition was concerned with social exclusion (Jordan 1996) and thought that *social exclusion* is a good alternative term. Though there is no clear record of how the term *social exclusion* came into use in English-language policy contexts, it made its English-language debut in the European Union poverty programs in the 1980s (Peace 2001). The term *exclusion sociale* in French or *social exclusion* in English offered an alternative that avoids the stigma of such terms as *poverty* and *deprivation.*

Defining social exclusion has proved to be elusive. From the existing literature, we can formulate that social exclusion occurs when individuals are unable to participate in any of the key economic, social, and political activities of a society in which they live. The factors that prevent an individual from participating in the economic, social, and political activities of a society could be a lack of resources, insufficient financial means, or inadequate social networks.

Humans belong to various groups, from families to nations. The collective action of these groups shelters those at the risk of social exclusion. In the case of a nation, citizenship provides necessary inclusion. According to Jordan (1996), the poor are excluded because they are unable to make the relevant contribution to groups that can provide collective economic action to shelter them from poverty. These groups could be social networks through which a person might find information to get a job. Some individuals also face social exclusion because they have fewer capacities and resources, for example, children, the elderly, and persons with a disability.

Persons or institutions occupying a strategic social position in society have the power to deprive certain people (the less qualified, immigrants, the homeless, etc.) of certain social commodities (such as employment, housing, education, income, status, power) and to create social exclusion (Vranken 1996). In this sense, social exclusion may be seen as exclusion from social networks that can provide access to social commodities. This does not mean that the poor are without social networks. The poor do have social networks, but unlike networks of the non-poor, these provide little or no access to the important social commodities—such as a job—that can help them escape poverty.

Several types of exclusion have been identified in the European social policy literature. These include social marginalization, democratic political exclusion, legal exclusion, exclusion from the "minimal acceptable way of life," cultural exclusion (including exclusion based on race and gender), exclusion from family, exclusion from the community, exclusion from the welfare state, exclusion from mainstream political and economic life, the state of deprivation, detachment from work relations, economic exclusion,

exclusion from the labour market, and poverty (Peace 2001). Clearly, *exclusion* is a loaded term that refers to many traits of poverty. Sen, a Nobel laureate economist, believes that poverty analysis can substantially benefit from the insights of the social exclusion perspective (Sen 2000). He identifies the following six types of social exclusion in modern societies:

1. Inequality and Poverty: The social exclusion may happen if some people become poor due to a sudden reversal in economic growth. For example, economic growth changed into economic decline in East and Southeast Asia in 1990s and many people became poor.
2. Labour Market Exclusion: Institutions of slavery and bounded-labour curtail the freedom to participate in the labour market and enforce exclusion of the poor from the labour market.
3. Credit Market Exclusion: Denial of access to credit based on lower income by financial institutions is a form of exclusion of the poor from the credit market.
4. Gender Related Exclusions and Inequality: Persistent inequality between men and women and exclusion of women from employment opportunities, education, and training are the main reasons of poverty among women in many societies. Inadequate policies related to the balancing of family and work responsibilities, child care, and maternity leave may exclude women from labour market opportunities leaving them at the risk of poverty.
5. Health Care: The exclusion of the poor from public health services provided by the state is a reality in most societies. The exclusion from public health care may result because of unavailability of modern health care in the poorer regions and high medicinal cost.
6. Food and Poverty: The poor are excluded from the food market when they are unable to buy food because of high prices.

Conclusion

No single one of the above perspectives can fully explain why poverty remains so pervasive in affluent societies such as Canada. Culturists argue that society fails to provide social, political, and economic organization to the low-income population and that the poor therefore develop alternative social institutions. Culturists also argue that traits such as fear of authority, fatalism, and suspicion of the institutions of the majority society are outcomes of the poor's isolation from mainstream society. Situationalists contend that the poor believe in middle-class values but that they behave differently from the middle class because of the unavailability of means to achieve economic success. Waxman (1977) argues that the stigma of poverty isolates the poor from mainstream society. The perspective of social exclusion contends that because some groups are deprived of important social commodities, such as education, employment, and housing, they become poor.

We can conclude that exclusion from the social and economic institutions of mainstream society deprives the poor of potential sources of income. The poor's segregation from sources of income may result from a range of different reasons, not exclusively from either culture, environment, social exclusion, or stigma. It could be a combination of any of these factors. The cause of segregation could be geographical isolation, discrimination, or inadequate financial support. The segregation of the poor from the institutions of the majority society creates a barrier for the transfer of skills and technology required to qualify for a job in an industrial society.

In other words, there are some intervening factors between the poor and mainstream society that limit their access to social and economic institutions. These intervening factors keep the poor from earning a standard of living that will allow them to live above the poverty level and are thus the reasons for their isolation. And while these reasons may vary, the outcome is the same: the poor fail to attain their full economic potential. Poverty imposes serious constraints on children in obtaining an education. The lack of daycare services hinders a single mother from joining the workforce because she instead needs to remain at home to take care of her children. The elderly working in jobs without an employer's pension have to stop working at some point and then live off a state pension alone. A member of an ethnic group may not realize his or her full economic potential because society condones ethnic discrimination. Recent immigrants may suddenly find that the same skills that earned them a decent living in their place of origin are not recognized by the professional or occupational organizations of their new country. Some geopolitical realities may isolate an entire region or community from potential economic resources, as is the case with the reserve system for Canada's First Nations.

Equally, society may organize the structure of power in such a way that impedes integration of the poor into the political and economic institutions of the society. At another extreme, the poor are relegated to such institutions of exclusion as prison, halfway houses, and mental institutions. These institutions further reinforce segregation of the poor from the mainstream society. It is not difficult to conclude from the foregoing discussion that full participation by the poor in the economic and social institutions of the society is a necessity to ameliorate their conditions of poverty.

Chapter 2

Ethnic Poverty

Introduction

Unlike in many developing countries, in developed countries such as Canada poverty is not a problem of the population at large. Instead, it is restricted to people within specific demographic groups, such as certain ethnic groups, the elderly, single mothers, and recent immigrants. Ethnic groups may be physically identifiable (e.g., black people, South-Asian people, or Aboriginal peoples) or they may be culturally different from the dominant group members or from each other (e.g., Italians, Greeks, and Jews). Strictly speaking, physically identifiable groups are termed *racial groups*, and culturally identifiable groups are termed *ethnic groups*. However, because racial groups may also be culturally identifiable, in this book we use the term *ethnic group* for both racially identifiable groups and culturally identifiable groups.

A group becomes economically disadvantaged when it is unable to participate in the social and economic institutions of society as a result of exclusion. The main cause of ethnic poverty is social exclusion based on racial and ethnic discrimination. To understand the dynamics among discrimination, ethnic poverty, and ethnic social exclusion, it is important to first understand the sociological concepts of assimilation (integration) and segregation. Assimilation and integration are opposite terms to social exclusion. The most popular and influential concept continues to be Gordon's 1964 model of assimilation. This model is based on the experience of immigrants in the United States, Australia, Canada, and New Zealand. Gordon (1964) speaks of three processes of assimilation. The first is Anglo-conformity; that is, to conform to the dominant Anglo-Saxon values. This has taken place in the United States; Australia; New Zealand; and, to some extent, Canada. The second of Gordon's processes of assimilation is called the melting pot, where all cultures in a country give rise to a new, synthetic culture. In the case of the melting pot, along with cultural assimilation, there is biological assimilation through intermarriage. This form of assimilation characterized European immigrants in the United States. Gordon's third process of assimilation is cultural-pluralism, or multiculturalism, where assimilation by the host society is not sought by integration at the primary level (i.e., by intermarriage), but is instead accomplished by the co-operation of various groups at the secondary level—that is, seeking full participation in political, economic, and civic institutions. These are the aims of multiculturalism, which is the official policy of Canada. It is part of the Canadian Charter of Rights and Freedoms, which is enshrined in the Canadian constitution. To promote inclusion and equality, and to forbid discrimination on ethnic, racial, or religious grounds, Canada has also adopted the Canadian Human Rights Act, the Employment Equity Act, and the Multiculturalism Act.

Minority Status and Discrimination

An ethnic minority group may remain isolated from mainstream society as a result of prejudice. Prejudice is a prejudgment that implies that all members of a given minority uniformly possess certain characteristics. In psychology, racial or ethnic prejudice is defined as an emotional, relatively inflexible, and categorical antipathy toward the members of a minority group, individually or collectively. Prejudice can exist as an attitudinal phenomenon at either an individual or a group level.

Prejudice as a cultural phenomenon

But prejudice does not occur only at an attitudinal level. It is also a cultural phenomenon. The habits of discrimination against minorities can be learnt through socialization, just like other habits and preferences. Parents or peer groups may indoctrinate the prevailing practices of discrimination that exist in their community. Prejudice that leads to discrimination has the effect of segregating members of a minority group from the mainstream society and eventually excluding them from the social and economic opportunities available in the society. In this way, prejudice leading to discrimination is a main cause of the social exclusion of some ethnic groups. This exclusion deprives those ethnic groups of access to the economic institutions of the society that are a potential source of income. We can only fully appreciate society's capacity to exclude poor ethnic groups from the social and economic institutions of the dominant society once we understand the power structure in a society.

Exclusion, Minority Status, and Power

In sociological parlance, people who do not hold power and who suffer systemic discrimination are called a minority. The population of a minority group can be large or small; it is not the numbers but the concept of power that is basic to the study of minority groups in sociology. Power is defined as an ability to control the behaviour of others, even in the absence of their consent (Robertson 1977, 566). Not only wealth, but also power is unequally distributed in most societies. In democratic societies, the extension of voting right to minorities is usually interpreted as a broadening of the power base. However, progress in the distribution of power through voting is often offset by the growth of government bureaucracy and powerful corporate interests. As a result, even in democratic societies, power becomes concentrated at the upper level of the executive branches of government and the corporate economy. Traditionally, those with political power in Canada tended to be white, middle-aged, male, Protestant, and, perhaps most significantly, wealthy (Armitage 1988). Though change in political power is visible, this is still true as Canadian legislatures are mostly dominated by white, male, and non-poor persons.

Racism and Ethnic Stratification in Canada

As defined by Richmond (1988, 190), racism is an ideology that either asserts genetic superiority of one population over another or affirms a set of attitudes, values, behaviours, or institutions that directly or indirectly discriminate against or systemically disadvantage a minority defined in terms of race. Prejudice and discrimination are important components of racism that hinder the full social and economic participation of a minority group against which racism is directed. In other words, racism supports social exclusion of minority groups. According to Richmond (1988, 22), racism is deeply embedded in the institutional structure of Western societies and has been internalized in the personalities of those who work within and through these institutions. The Parliamentary committee on "visible minorities" in Canada reported the existence of racism in employment and promotion system in the public and private sector, immigration control procedures, the administration of justice, the education system, and the mass media (Richmond 1988, 133). A recent study by Satzewich (2011) provides a detailed analysis of racism in Canada. While acknowledging its complexity, he believes that racism exists in Canada but is not a widespread and fundamental feature of the society.

Few societies are completely stratified based on the ethnic attributes of its members. But most societies are ethnically stratified to some extent in that different ethnic groups are socially classified, ranked, and evaluated. Ethnicity is an important predictor of a person's life chances in an ethnically stratified society. Members of such a society can foresee the kinds of jobs they will get, the types of schools their children will attend, and the amount of wealth they will amass in their lifetime. The majority usually has a monopoly over power, privilege, and prestige. The majority may promote or provide a "moral" rationale for its racist ideology against the minority group in order to maintain its position of dominance, and it may also justify its super-ordinate position in the social and economic system.

The presence of ethnic stratification in Canada was first documented by Porter (1965) in his work on the "ethnic mosaic." He found Aboriginal peoples (First Nations people and Inuit) at the bottom of the Canadian social ladder. According to Harding (1965), historically in Canada, racism toward First Nations peoples has taken the form of paternalistic policies propagated to protect "childlike" peoples incapable of managing their own affairs. The provision of self-government to Aboriginal peoples of Canada that is discussed at the end of the chapter is a response by the Canadian government to this criticism.

Ethnic Minorities in Poverty in Canada

Two groups in Canada often cited in the literature of ethnic poverty are recent immigrants and Aboriginal peoples.

Recent immigrants

The Canadian Council on Social Development published results of its study on the labour market experience and incomes of recent immigrants in 1995 and 1998 (Smith and Jackson 2002). The study reports that the poverty rate of 27 percent in 1998 for recent immigrants was double the 13 percent rate for the rest of the Canadian population and that their annual wages and salaries were one-third less than those of rest of the Canadians.

Poverty among recent immigrants is an important concern because Human Resources and Skills Development Canada (2002) expects that from 2011 onward, immigration will account for virtually all of the net growth in the Canadian labour force. The aging of the European populations has reduced European immigration to Canada. Currently, the main sources for immigration to Canada are predominantly non-European countries. Because people from many of these source countries are visible minorities, government's anti-racism policies are pivotal to combat poverty among recent immigrants. In the Canadian census, visible minorities are defined as "persons, other than Aboriginal peoples, who are non-Caucasian in race or non-white in colour." The term *visible minority* thus defined is somewhat confusing, but it is used not only in Canada's Employment Equity Act but also in the census. The 2006 census revealed that 1 in 6 Canadians belong to a visible minority group. The visible minority population in Canada is likely to increase because future immigrants are also likely to come from non-European countries. Moreover, Canada will continue to seek immigrants to renew its labour force and refurbish its population because its birth rate is likely to stay below the replacement level.

Despite the implementation of the Canadian Charter of Rights and Freedoms, the Canadian Human Rights Act, the Employment Equity Act, and the Multiculturalism Act, a large gap exists in the actual social and economic outcomes among people from different racial and ethnic groups in Canada (Smith and Jackson 2002).

The most important mark of success of Canada's multiculturalism policy would be the successful inclusion of immigrants in the Canadian labour force. The experience that immigrants gain through labour force participation is important for their future social and economic mobility and for their inclusion in the Canadian society. Recent immigrants, particularly recent visible minority immigrants, have not only high unemployment rates but also high underemployment rates because a large proportion of them are employed in low-wage jobs that often do not match their skills and formal credentials (Smith and Jackson 2002). Another study reported that the poverty rate (defined in terms of Statistics Canada's low income cut-off) in 1995 was 52 percent among immigrants who arrived in 1991, up from 35 percent among those who arrived in 1986 (Lee 2000). Once immigrants are in Canada, their poverty rate declines over time. If this phenomenon reverses, an unknown number of recent immigrants could fall into a long-term poverty leading to intergeneration poverty.

The economic success of immigrants is directly related to the social mobility of second-generation Canadians. Poverty of parents often leads to inadequate schooling of children, which may lead to poorly paid employment when they grow up to be adults. Therefore, the policies that seek economic inclusion of immigrants in Canadian society are very important for the prevention of intergenerational poverty. According to Smith and Jackson (2002), despite high levels of formal education among many recent visible minority immigrants, a very large gap exists between their earnings and those of other Canadians. This gap is much smaller or non-existent for Canadian-born visible minority persons, which indicates that there are some other factors apart from discrimination that play a part in the low earnings of recent immigrants in Canada. Non-recognition or under-evaluating of foreign credentials and an inability of employers to use the skills of those with good language skills are part of the reasons for poor labour market outcomes of recent immigrants in Canada (Smith and Jackson 2002).

During economic slowdown, new entrants into the job market face difficulty in finding steady, well-paying work. This is particularly so for new immigrants because employers may exhibit more discriminatory behaviour in their hiring decisions during a slowdown than during an economic recovery. Yet, there is evidence that even if Canada's economy is growing strongly, for example, between 1993 and 1998, large gaps between the earnings of recent immigrants and other Canadians prevailed (Smith and Jackson 2002). This indicates that economic recovery alone is not sufficient to achieve equality in the workforce for recent immigrants. Elimination of labour market discrimination is also important.

Immigrants: Poverty and labour market experience and discrimination

Structural and institutional discrimination is most difficult to eradicate because it seems to be unintentional. For example, the major hiring criteria in the workplaces of a free enterprise society should be education and experience. However, Henry and Ginzberg (1984) reported the existence of racism in hiring practices in Canada, even after controlling for education, years of experience, and age. For the purposes of their study, they defined discrimination as "those practices or attitudes, wilful or unintentional, which have the effect of limiting an individual's right to economic opportunities because of irrelevant traits such as skin colour, ethnic background, or accent." To gather the data, Henry and Ginzberg used two tests: in the first, applicants similar in age, sex, education, and employment histories were asked to answer advertisements for jobs listed in a major Toronto newspaper to determine how resumés with ethnic-looking names and foreign credentials would be treated by the potential employers; in the second test, the job applicants were asked to telephone potential employers, to see how employers treated applicants with non-Canadian accents and with ethnic-sounding names.

The study found that the most significant amount of discrimination was directed at Indo-Pakistanis, who in 44 percent of the cases were told that jobs were no longer available. This percentage was 36 for black West Indians, 31 for white immigrants with Italian or Slavic accents, and only 13 for the white Canadians (Henry and Ginzberg 1984). Though a similar study has not been replicated in Canada again, unfavourable workforce experience of visible minorities and recent immigrants described by recent studies (Richmond 1988; Kelly 1995; Reitz 2005) suggests that visible minorities still experience discrimination in job market.

A Statistics Canada study (Kelly 1995) shows that visible minorities in Canada are far more educated than the rest of the population and are concentrated in the prime working ages (25 to 44), yet they experience higher levels of unemployment and underemployment. This study further reports that a larger proportion of visible minorities is employed in low-paying clerical, service, and manual labour jobs. Even visible minorities of prime working age with a university degree are less likely than their non-visible-minority counterparts to be employed in professional or managerial occupations.

Data in an atlas of what was then called the Ontario Ministry of Culture and Recreation (1982) showed that, although among Indo-Pakistanis the percentage of university degree holders was more than four times higher than that among the total population in 1971 and more than double in 1976 than the total population, the unemployment rate in this ethnic group remained double that of the total population. These data tally with the findings of the report by Henry and Ginzberg (1984). In most industrialized countries, unemployment is negatively correlated with education. However, in Canada, numerous studies confirm that during the first few years after their arrival in Canada, immigrants experience higher than average unemployment and also face serious underemployment relative to their skills and qualifications (Ornstein and Sharma 1983; Sharma 1981a, 1981b; Clodman and Richmond 1981). The higher levels of underemployment and unemployment, and hence poverty, is likely be on account of discrimination in the labour market as reported in the Henry and Ginzberg study (1984).

According to the perspective of functional theory, most members of a free enterprise capitalist society would support stratification if criteria of experience, education, and competence were fairly applied in hiring and promotions. The deliberate violation of these criteria by the dominant group can generate frustration, anger, and distrust among the members of a minority group toward the majority group. This in turn can lead to mental and social problems in the minority group and conflict in the society as a whole. Ethnic conflicts in society propagate ethnic segregation (Richmond 1988). Ethnic segregation, in turn, leads to social exclusion of ethnic minorities, which is the main cause of long-term poverty among ethnic minorities in many societies.

Basavarajappa and Verma (1985), in their analysis of data on Asian immigrants in Canada in the 1981 census, found that a higher proportion of recently arrived families lived below the poverty line (low income cut-off). They examined their data to test hypotheses on assimilation and the minority group status. The minority group status hypothesis was put forward to explain the lower earnings of black people in the United States.

The assimilation hypothesis states that the majority of immigrants enter the labour force at a low socio-economic status (SES) level and gradually converge toward the socio-economic status of the dominant group as they become culturally and structurally assimilated (Park 1950; Gordon 1964; Jackson 1970), and that closeness in linguistic, cultural, and racial characteristics of immigrants to the host society increases the propensity of their assimilation process. In other words, for immigrants with linguistic, cultural, and racial characteristics similar to the host society, as the length of residence in the host society increases, the differences between the minority group and the dominant group gradually reduce and eventually disappear. However, those ethnic groups that differ with respect to these characteristics are likely to remain in a lower socio-economic status level beyond the first generation (Porter 1965). Basavarajappa and Verma (1985) found some support for the assimilation hypothesis in their study.

The minority group status hypothesis states that differences in socio-economic status between the minority group and the dominant group will persist even with parity in educational and occupation levels. The differences are attributed to discrimination and ethnic culture. Ethnic culture refers to the fact that the minority status of a group might result in its members having values (such as fatalism) that prevent them from competing successfully with the dominant group. Sandefur and Scott (1983); Richmond (1979); and Henry and Ginzberg (1984) found evidence of discrimination against black people and Asians in Toronto. Beaujot, Basavarajappa, and Verma (1988) reported that a higher proportion of the cohorts of pre-1975 immigrants and the recent immigrants remained below the poverty line (low income cut-offs). The same study also reported that lower proportions of immigrants from the United Kingdom and Northern Europe were below the poverty line. These findings suggest that the higher proportion of newly arrived immigrants below the poverty line in Canada can be explained by the minority group status hypothesis.

The findings of the studies of the early 1980s that revealed higher levels of underemployment and unemployment among immigrants (Sharma 1981a, 1981b; Ornstein and Sharma 1983) were still tenable in the 2000s in Canada. Reitz (2005) found that foreign-trained immigrants were better educated than native-born Canadians, yet they had a difficult time in finding work in areas they were trained in, and their incomes were falling further and further behind. Reitz's (2005) study reported that in 1980, on average, newly arrived immigrant men earned about 80 percent of the average salary of native-born Canadians. Twenty years later, in 2000, they earned only 60 percent of the average salary of native-born Canadians, and they were more likely to be unemployed, even at a menial job. The study revealed that while in 1980 more than 86 percent of immigrant men compared with 91 percent of Canadian-born men were employed, in 2000 only 68 percent of newcomers compared with 85 percent of the Canadian-born adults had jobs.

Reitz (2005) further warns that those immigrants who are denied work in the knowledge occupations often wind up in the least-skilled occupations, while high-skilled jobs in Canada go unfilled. According to Reitz (2005), this vicious circle creates heightened competition even for menial jobs. Immigrants living in poverty may thus create pressure, or at least the perception of pressure, on the social safety net. The public perception that immigrants are a liability or a social problem may become widespread and could lead to public demands for reduction in social programs (Reitz 2005). Because social integration is linked to employment (as we saw earlier), this analysis leads to a conclusion that new immigrants to Canada are experiencing social exclusion that for many of them could lead to long-term poverty. Because Canada's population is aging, it needs immigration for its labour force renewal; a backlash against immigration in Canada could potentially lead to the stagnation of Canada's economy and exacerbate economic problems associated with population decline.

A Statistics Canada study (3 February 2005) on home ownership further validates Reitz's concerns. It reports that home ownership rates among working-age immigrant families in Montreal and Toronto exceeded those of their Canadian-born counterparts in 1981. But the situation was reversed in 2001. In the intervening 20 years, the home ownership rate for immigrant families declined from 52 percent to 42 percent in Montreal and from 65 percent to 61 percent in Toronto, while for Canadian-born families the rate of home ownership increased from 46 percent to 54 percent in Montreal and from 55 percent to 64 percent in Toronto. The study found that some of this decline in home ownership is linked to the dramatic decline in the success of immigrants in the labour market, which in turn may be linked to shifts in the immigration source countries, an increase in visible minorities among immigrants, and the emergence of ethnic enclaves in these two Canadian cities.

Emergence of ethnic enclaves

The expression "the emergence of ethnic enclaves" is a euphemism for ghettoization. There was no evidence of ghettoization in Metropolitan Toronto in 1980 (Sharma 1982b). Yet by 2001, the United Way of Greater Toronto reported 120 ghettos in Toronto (CTVNews, 5 April 2004). Kazemipur and Halli (2000) examined an ethnic dimension to Canadian poverty and found a rising trend in ghettoization of ethnic groups in Canada during the

1990s. They reported that certain ethnic groups, especially visible minorities and recent immigrants, suffered from poverty due to economic as well as other factors, including limited knowledge of the official languages and a mismatch of their skills with the occupations in demands in the labour market. The geographical and economic exclusion of ethnic groups is a first step to other social problems, such as decay of inner cities and the kinds of inter-ethnic or inter-racial conflicts seen in the United States, England, and France.

Not racially but culturally different immigrants

In fact, every wave of immigrants in Canada has experienced discrimination, and each had their story to tell. Let me give you an example. In 1981, I was hired into the Ontario Public Service by a Polish man named Rudolf Kogler. One day, when Rudy and I were having dinner in a small restaurant in Ottawa, he struck up a conversation with me on ethnic discrimination by stating, "It is much better for you guys now." I was surprised that a white man like Rudy would have faced discrimination as an immigrant. I asked him, "What do you mean?" I still vividly recall his response.

> After World War II, I got a scholarship and did M.A. in economics from St. Andrews University in Scotland. After the graduation, I moved to London to search for a job. I went to an Employment Exchange Office. The lady looked at my certificates and told me that there are no positions for economists. When I asked what kind of positions were available, she said that there was a position of an orderly in a hospital.
>
> Failing to find any job suitable for my qualifications, I went to a construction company and told the contractor that I did construction work in the army. The contractor could see my lie on my face. He lifted my opened palms in his hands and then said sarcastically, "I know you did construction! But I like your face and will offer you a job". He gave me a paper which I had to get approved from the Employment Exchange office. I went back to the same employment office and told the officer that I needed to get this document approved. He saw the salary, which was much higher than that of a hospital orderly. He refused to sign the paper and told me that a job with this kind of salary was for British and you cannot get this job. I got furious and told him that I was a captain in the army, I commanded British troops; I fought for this country in the deserts of Libya and swamps of Italy. If you did not sign this paper, I would

see my MP and complain. He signed the paper and I became a construction worker in London with two Masters degrees, one from Poland and one from Scotland, I worked as a construction worker for five years in London. If you happened to be in Trafalgar Square or Piccadilly Circus, I bet that you would step on a brick laid by me. After five years, I decided that it was enough of manual work. I still had zeal to work as an economist. At that time, Poles were migrating to Canada.

I went to the Canadian High Commission in London and completed an application to migrate to Canada. The immigration officer asked my occupation and I told him that I was an economist and had an M.A. in economics. He said that there were no jobs available for economists in Canada. Then, after six months I went to Canadian immigration office in a small town. This time I told the immigration officer that I was a construction worker. You would not believe, three companies were fighting to recruit me. One was in Lethbridge, one in Toronto, and one in Winnipeg. I chose Toronto because many Poles were already settled in Toronto. I landed in Toronto in 1952. But it was impossible to find a job of an economist. Sears would hire a Polish person; but never in sales or on a front desk but behind the public eye in their warehouse. I started working in Sears warehouse. One night while cleaning the floor, I saw an advertisement for a statistical assistant. Longing to move on to a white collar job, I applied for the position. I was told that I had an accent. I did not get the job that required only number skill. I had a degree from the United Kingdom which meant I knew English. Finally, Government of Ontario needed an economist to analyze demographic data from 1956 census. I had taken courses in demography in my M.A. program at the St. Andrews University. During those days it was hard to get an economist with demographic training as Canada did not have demographic program in its universities in the 1950s. Therefore, I got the job in 1961. Now, I will soon turn 65 and with working years not enough for a full pension. You see that is why I thought it is easier for today's new comers like you.

One could get the impression from the earlier discussion that discrimination in Canada historically has been directed toward only those who were racially different, such as visible minorities or Aboriginal Canadians, but Rudy's story shows that even white people experienced discrimination simply because they were culturally different. Of course, during those 10 years between when Rudy landed and when he finally got a job in his field, there was no Human Rights Act, no Canadian Charter of Rights and Freedoms. However, even today, in spite of these statutory protections, recent immigrants face experiences that are not very different from those faced by Rudy. And statutory protections are meaningless in practical terms for poor recent immigrants: they cannot fight discrimination in courts of law because to fight a legal case you need money, and to have money you need a job.

Canada's Aboriginal Population: Exclusion and Poverty

This chapter explores the dimension of ethnic poverty in Canada in the light of institutional segregation and discrimination. In the following sections, we will elaborate on the problem of ethnic poverty and social exclusion in connection with Aboriginal peoples in Canada. It is worth beginning with a comparison of several demographic, health, social, and economic conditions.

In the 2006 census, 1,172,790 people (or 3.8 percent of the Canadian population) identified themselves as Aboriginal. The proportion of Aboriginal peoples in the population had increased by 46 percent since 1996, whereas the population of Canada had grown by only 8 percent. The census identified three groups of Aboriginal peoples, as follows:

1. First Nations: includes status Indians registered under the Indian Act and non-status Indians who are not registered for the purposes of the Indian Act.
2. Métis: descendants of people of mixed Aboriginal and European ancestry.
3. Inuit: a distinct cultural group who generally live north of the tree line.

The census revealed that among over a million Aboriginal Canadians, nearly 62 percent were First Nations, approximately 34 percent were Métis, and the remaining 4 percent were Inuit. Aboriginal peoples were quite unevenly distributed across the country. Aboriginal peoples made up almost 85 percent of the population in Nunavut, 50 percent in the Northwest Territories, and 25 percent in Yukon. For the rest of the country, the numbers were 15 percent in Manitoba and Saskatchewan, 5 percent in Alberta, British Columbia, and Newfoundland and Labrador; and less than 3 percent in the remaining provinces.

A glance at some of the important demographic, health, education, socio-economic, and administration of justice statistics for Aboriginal peoples in Canada indicates that conditions of poverty among them are as pervasive as they are in some developing countries.

Aboriginal Demographic and Health Indicators

High birth rate and younger population

The total fertility rate (the number of births per woman) of 2.6 for Aboriginal woman is 65 percent higher than that of Canadian women as a whole. Because of this high fertility rate, people are younger and families are larger, on average, than in the non-Aboriginal population. The median age of the Aboriginal population is 27 years, compared with 40 years for Canada as a whole. Almost 28 percent of Inuit children, 25 percent of First Nations children, and 11 percent of Métis children live in families with four or more children, compared with 8 percent of non-Aboriginal children.

Mortality and life expectancy

The life expectancy (i.e., the average age a person may expect to live) of the Aboriginal population is considerably lower than that of the Canadian population as a whole because of high levels of mortality among Aboriginal peoples. Demographers use life expectancy as an indicator of the social well-being of a society. The lower life expectancies of Aboriginal peoples compared with the rest of the Canadian population indicates that the Aboriginal population lives in poor socio-economic and health conditions. According to Statistics Canada (2006a), in 2001, the life expectancy at birth for Canada overall was 77.0 years for men and 82.2 years for women. For First Nations peoples, it was estimated to be 71.1 years for men and 76.7 years for women. The life expectancy of 62.6 years for men and 71.7 years for women among the Inuit was the lowest among the three Aboriginal groups. The life expectancy of Aboriginal groups ranged between 5 to 14 years lower than the general Canadian population, and matched the levels that were attained a quarter-century earlier by Canadians as whole.

Statistics Canada (1 February 2005) reported that a community predominantly populated by Aboriginal peoples, the Région de Nunavik in Quebec, has the lowest life expectancy in Canada, at 66.7 years. This places Région de Nunavik between the Dominican Republic and Egypt (note that the Dominican Republic ranked 111th and Egypt ranked 112th among 191 countries). In this report, Statistics Canada explains that the Canadian communities with the lowest life expectancies are in the most northern and isolated parts of Canada. People in these communities live on low incomes, and a high proportion of them depend on government transfer payments. Smoking, heavy drinking, and a high accident rate are also prevalent. Aboriginal peoples also die in larger numbers as a result of contagious diseases and suicide. The tuberculosis rate is 8 times higher than that of Canada as a whole (Department of Indian and Northern Development [DIAND] 2001). Suicide and self-injury are the leading causes of death for Aboriginal youths. Suicide accounts for 22 percent of all deaths among 10-to-19-year-olds and 16 percent of all deaths among 20-to-44-year-olds (Health Canada 2002a).

Aboriginal Social and Economic Indicators

Education

There are big differences in the educational attainment of Aboriginal and non-Aboriginal peoples in Canada. Levels of education are much lower among Aboriginal peoples. According to the 2006 census, 13 percent of the Canadian population as a whole have less than a high-school education, compared with 33 percent of the Aboriginal population. The differences are still greater in university education. Roughly 25 percent of non-Aboriginal adults have a university degree, compared with 9 percent of Métis and 7 percent of both First Nations peoples and Inuit.

Employment

The low educational attainment of the Aboriginal population is a predictor of poor employment outcomes. In 2006, the employment rate for Aboriginal peoples of core working age (25 to 54) was about 66 percent, compared with about 82 percent for non-Aboriginal peoples. The employment rate among First Nations peoples was 52 percent for those living on-reserve and 66 percent for those living off-reserve. The employment rate was 61 percent for Inuit and about 75 percent for Métis. Another aspect of Aboriginal employment was that it was seasonal in nature because Aboriginal peoples were more likely to be in traditional, seasonal occupations, such as fishing, trapping, forestry, or logging.

The occupational structure of the Aboriginal population is also conducive to the conditions of poverty. The Canadian Human Rights Commission analyzed employment equity data from private and public sector employers and found that First Nations peoples were drastically under-represented in virtually every industrial sector and occupation (Speirs 1989).

Families

A relatively higher proportion of Aboriginal families are headed by single parents. Female lone-parent families are twice as common among Aboriginal peoples than among non-Aboriginal Canadians. Aboriginal families also have more children, and Aboriginal households are more likely to include such relatives as the parents' parents, married children, grandparents, aunts, uncles, and cousins. These relatives make up 6 percent of the Aboriginal household population, in contrast to only 2 percent of non-Aboriginal households. Whereas, in non-Aboriginal households, an increase in the number of people results in an increase in the average income, in Aboriginal households it does not. According to the 2006 census, the average income of $21,300 for a five-person Aboriginal household decreases to $19,700 for an eight-person household.

Aboriginal children under the age of 15 are more likely than non-Aboriginal children to live with their grandparents, with neither of their parents present in the household. The 2006 Census reported that 3 percent of First Nations children and 2 percent of both Inuit and Métis children were living with their grandparents, as compared with only 0.4 percent of non-Aboriginal children.

Six percent of registered First Nations children were placed away from parental care to protect them from neglect or abuse, compared with less than 1 percent of Canadian children as a whole (DIAND 2001). On reserves, registered First Nations people see a lack of education, drug and alcohol abuse, poverty, and psychological issues as the most important challenges facing Aboriginal children and youth (DIAND 2001). These social problems among Aboriginal children and youth are the result of pervasive and enduring conditions of poverty, and they encourage social exclusion of Aboriginal children and perpetuate poverty from one generation to the next.

Housing

Housing conditions are another indicator of socio-economic status. According to the 2006 census, only 7 percent of non-Aboriginal homes required major repairs, compared with 29 percent of First Nations, 26 percent of Métis, and 28 percent of Inuit homes. Again according to the 2006 census, 45 percent of First Nations homes on-reserve and 17 percent of homes off-reserve needed major repairs. Aboriginal homes were also more likely to be crowded. A dwelling is said to be crowded in Canada when it contains more than one person per room. Overall, Aboriginal peoples were four times more likely to live in crowded dwelling conditions than were non-Aboriginal peoples (Statistics Canada 2008).

Income

Low income is a reality for the Aboriginal population. In 2005, Aboriginal peoples on average earned two-thirds as much as non-Aboriginal peoples.

According to the 2006 census, the average annual income for Aboriginal persons 25 to 54 years old was $22,000, whereas the average income for non-Aboriginal persons of the same age was $33,000. The average income of First Nations peoples was $19,000, followed by Inuit, with an average income just below $25,000, and Métis, with an average income of $28,000. The average income of First Nations peoples living off-reserve was about $22,500, whereas that of peoples living on-reserve was only $14,000. The larger family size and the low-income level indicate that a large proportion of this minority lives in poverty.

Administration of justice

Historically, Aboriginal peoples have been over-represented in the Canadian justice system. A 1988 Canadian Human Rights Commission (CHRC) report pointed out that although Aboriginal peoples make up only 2 percent of the Canadian population, 10 percent of males and 13 percent of females in federal penitentiaries are Aboriginal (Speirs 1989). Aboriginal peoples are also over-represented in adult correctional services institutions (i.e., provincial and territorial prisons). Aboriginal adults represented 21 percent of admissions to provincial and territorial correctional facilities, and 18 percent of admissions to federal facilities in 2002–03 (Statistics Canada 6 June 2006). Among the provinces, the highest proportions of Aboriginal correctional admissions were in the Prairie provinces, where Aboriginal peoples make up a high proportion of the population. Among those admitted to provincially sentenced custody, 80 percent were Aboriginal in Saskatchewan, 68 percent in Manitoba, and 39 percent in Alberta (Statistics Canada 6 June 2006). According to the CHRC report (Speirs 1989), First Nations youth in Canada have a better chance of being sent to prison than of completing a university education.

But Aboriginal peoples are not only over-represented in the correctional system, they are also more likely to be the victim of crime. According to Statistics Canada (6 June 2006), Aboriginal peoples were three times more likely than non-Aboriginal peoples to be the victim of violent crime—specifically, sexual assault, robbery, and physical assault.

All these social and economic conditions limit Aboriginal peoples' participation in Canadian society, a participation that is imperative for earning incomes to rise above the poverty level. The causes for low socio-economic conditions and poor health indicators of Aboriginal peoples are intertwined with Canadian history, racism, and their minority status.

The following analysis of the literature on Aboriginal peoples in Canada provides some major causes of Aboriginal poverty, without resorting to blaming the people involved.

The Causes of Poverty among Aboriginal Peoples

There are many explanations as to why Aboriginal peoples in Canada lag behind in the economic race and experience persistent poverty. Some of the historical causes cited in the literature are colonial status, impact of dominant values, the relationship of power structure to the minority status, racism, and social exclusion.

Colonial history

Historically, First Nations peoples have been treated and controlled by the outside authority, just like happens with the colonized in any colonial society (Harding 1965). The First Nations reserves were created in the 1800s by the federal government when European settlement expanded in Canada with the help of railways. Those who agreed to the rights of reserve lost their rights to land (Frideres 1974). According to Harding (1965), originally reserves were established to concentrate the First Nations population in the hope that in addition to trapping, hunting, fishing, and corn horticulture, the reserves would enable First Nations peoples to develop an agricultural economy of their own. The authorities of that time assumed that once they had developed an agricultural economy, the next natural stage would be to develop an industrial economy. They anticipated the integration of the First Nations economy into the Canadian economy through a natural course of development—a hunting and trapping economy leading to an agricultural economy, and that agricultural economy progressing to an industrial economy. As it turned out, the reserve system failed to generate enough income, and it isolated First Nations people from the potential source of income—that is, Canadian society.

This failure of the reserves to provide income to the expanding populations of First Nations peoples, as well as their geographical isolation, became the major factors of their poverty. The prolonged exclusion of the First Nations population since the 1800s not only hampered the transfer of technology, it also created a large gap in educational levels between First Nations and the rest of the population. First Nations Canadians were isolated from mainstream life with limited ability to remain self-sufficient; when they relocated to urban areas, their dependence on welfare and their social exclusion did not diminish. This exclusion has also led to a loss of traditional skills, with Aboriginal peoples being forbidden from hunting, trapping, or fishing for the purpose of subsistence. As dependence increased, Aboriginal peoples lost touch with the traditional harvesting that is linked to rapport with the land and a sense of self-reliance

(Loppie-Reading and Wien 2009). The exclusion from voting is another example that elucidates the colonial status of Aboriginal peoples. They were legally restrained from voting until 1960, and band councils did not have the right to make by-laws about the internal affairs of their reserves (Harding 1965). These factors made them dependent on the federal government and prevented them from (re)gaining self-sufficiency. The isolation and colonial status of Aboriginal peoples had a deskilling effect. The isolation created by the reserve system and the ensuing social exclusion are responsible for the continued poverty among First Nations people of Canada.

Church-run, government-funded residential schools for Aboriginal children were supposed to prepare these children for life in white society. However, these attempts at assimilation through residential schools undermined culture, language, family ties, and community networks and had the effect of disengaging many Aboriginal peoples from their ancestry and cultural values (Loppie-Reading and Wien 2009). There were also widespread reports of physical, sexual, and emotional abuse. The most frequently reported experiences by the residential school survivors are isolation from their families, verbal or emotional abuse, harsh discipline, loss of cultural identity, separation from the community, witnessing abuse, loss of language, and experiencing physical abuse. These experiences not only contributed to depression, substance abuse, and social exclusion for the survivors of the abuse but also for their children. Among the children of survivors, 4 out of 10 believe that the residential school experience had a negative effect on the parenting skills of their parents (Loppie-Reading and Wien 2009).

Almost 40 percent of First Nations adults living on reserves reported experiencing racism (Loppie-Reading and Wien 2009). There is evidence from the research that when Aboriginal youth experience social exclusion, their alcohol and drug use increases (Mignone 2003, Mignone and O'Neil 2005). Substance abuse is associated with low self-esteem. From this, it is not difficult to conclude that racism-based social exclusion has a negative effect on the self-esteem of the victims. And low self-esteem further enhances social exclusion.

There have long been demands for acknowledgement and compensation. In 2007, two years after a compensation package was first announced, the Canadian government finally agreed to put it forth. Former residential school students were offered $10,000 for the first year or for the part of a year they attended school, plus $3,000 for each subsequent year (Loppie-Reading and Wien 2009). On 11 June 2008, Canadian prime minister Stephen Harper offered a full apology on behalf of Canadians for the Indian residential schools system.

The impact of dominant values

In an industrialized society with an effective communication network, it is common for the dominant values to spread throughout the various segments of the society. Even as early as 1956, Goodman's study provided evidence of such a phenomenon among the poor. The sociological literature also contends that the poor aspire to the material comforts of the middle class but that their economic situation limits these aspirations. This occasionally results in a frustration-aggression reaction and a generalized hostility toward the dominant group. Harding (1965) suggests that this phenomenon may have led to occasional frustration-aggression among First Nations peoples that in turn occasionally increased their hostility toward the Canadian establishment. This hostility may have further enhanced the isolation of First Nations peoples from the larger society.

Power and minority status

Power is related to the stratification system in a society. The roles performed by middle- and upper-class persons are more closely associated with the power structure of the society than those performed by lower-class persons. For example, a journalist would have more association with political power than an Aboriginal Canadian on social assistance living on-reserve because the socio-economic status of persons of Aboriginal heritage limits their association with the power structure of Canadian society. In essence, compared with a poor Aboriginal person, a middle-class journalist is more likely to vote, participate in elections, get elected to political office, and influence the political decision making through her or his writings.

A lack of power for an ethnic group also entails an inability to make decisions about their own welfare. Many Canadian scholars and politicians feel that a transfer of the power to make decisions may ameliorate the conditions of poverty among Aboriginal peoples in Canada over time. Since the 1980s, Aboriginal groups in Canada have progressively gained ground in establishing self-governance mechanisms. However, the process of removing conditions of poverty among Aboriginal peoples will be a long one because negotiations for self-government agreements between Aboriginal peoples and various levels of government take a long time.

Some agreements between the federal government and Aboriginal communities have been signed. Negotiations require a long span of time because self-government arrangements may take many forms due to the diverse historical, cultural, political, and economic circumstances of the Aboriginal groups, regions, and communities involved (Aboriginal Affairs and Northern Development Canada, 2012).

Self-government enables Aboriginal governments to work in partner-ship with other governments and the private sector to promote economic development and improve social conditions (INAC 2011). Achievement of self-government for Aboriginal peoples of Canada is the first step in acquir-ing control over their destiny.

Conceptual Explanation

What is the conceptual explanation for ethnic poverty? Because ethnic groups, such as various immigrant groups and Aboriginal peoples, belong to distinct cultures, it is tempting to seek an explanation under the frame-work of the culture of poverty. As was noted above, although recent im-migrants experience poverty in the beginning, most of them experience an improvement in their economic situation with the passage of time, and their income catches up with the native-born population. But the culture of poverty perspective is not very helpful in explaining poverty among re-cent immigrants who face a unique situation and environment in their new country. The structural conditions that are major roadblocks on the way to economic success for recent immigrants include poor communication skills, inadequate language training services in the host society, and lack of appropriate programs to help recent immigrants to integrate into the labour market and the social milieu of the new country. Policies aimed at improving language skills and recognizing the skills and credentials can go a long way toward social and economic integration of new immigrants. In this sense, the poverty of recent immigrants fits the situational perspective better than it does the culture of poverty perspective.

Social exclusion of recent immigrants is a real concern. The host society may use immigrants' unique culture, ethnic background, language, and ways of life as a basis for exclusion and deny them full participation in the key economic, social, and political activities. A lack of resources, financial means, and social networks also prevents recent immigrants from partici-pating in economic, social, and political activities. Policies and programs that enhance inclusion are immensely important to remove the barriers that exclude recent immigrants from the mainstream society and pose a threat of long-term poverty. Once excluded, immigrants fall prey to long-term poverty, and both they and the second generation are likely to expe-rience the stigma of poverty. The stigma of poverty affects self-worth and increases the possibility of intergenerational poverty taking root among immigrant communities. Therefore, effective settlement and inclusion policies are the key to save new immigrants from the poverty trap and to achieve the desired outcome of immigration—that is, keeping Canada prosperous and young.

The kind of ethnic poverty that is entrenched over a long period, such as poverty among Aboriginal peoples, is different from the kind of ethnic poverty faced by new immigrants. The most persistent poverty exists among the Aboriginal peoples of Canada, and it defies any one explanation. Discrimination, cultural prejudice, structural conditions, stigma, and, above all, social exclusion played a historical part in entrenching poverty among Canada's Aboriginal peoples. And in fact, nearly all conceptual perspectives developed to explain poverty could be applied to the conditions of poverty among Aboriginal Canadians.

Roach and Gursslin (1967) suggested that the concept of the culture of poverty should be applied to explain the behaviour of those poor who have lived in poverty for generations. Aboriginal peoples of Canada constitute distinct cultures and have lived in poverty for generations. They thus exhibit many traits described in the culture of poverty, such as an unprotected childhood, the fear of authority, fatalism, the suspicion of institutions, high prevalence of common-law unions, high rates of suicide, and high school dropout rates.

But the situational perspective might be equally appropriate to explain the high incidence of Aboriginal poverty in Canada. Before the arrival of Europeans in Canada, in spite of their relatively low technological level, Aboriginal peoples might have suffered abject poverty during lean times, but they would not have known the relative deprivation that depletes self-confidence and makes it difficult to break the poverty trap. As discussed earlier, demographic, social, economic, health, and education conditions of Aboriginal peoples of Canada create situations that are conducive to social exclusion. The social exclusion of Aboriginal peoples is reinforced by the geographical, social, and economic conditions in which they live. The prospect of self-government is likely to give the Aboriginal peoples back some of their self-esteem required for their self-sufficiency. Back in 1992, after many months of hearings, the Special Joint Committee on a Renewed Canada, popularly called the Beaudoin-Dobbie Committee, promised Aboriginal peoples the immediate right to "inherent" self-government (Special Joint Committee on a Renewed Canada 1992). Inherent self-government implies that Aboriginal peoples have held this right all along and have never given it up.

Today, Aboriginal Affairs and Northern Development Canada has a branch that manages the negotiation of practical and workable self-government arrangements with Aboriginal groups, provinces, and territories. The branch is also responsible for policy development and co-ordination of activities that support negotiations, strengthen Aboriginal governance, and develop new fiscal relationships with Aboriginal governments. Several Aboriginal groups have negotiated for Aboriginal governance, and other groups are already in the process of negotiations. When Aboriginal peoples are able to control their own destiny through self-government, the threat of social exclusion will diminish and social and economic well-being will improve.

Chapter 3

The Elderly in Poverty

Introduction

The population of the elderly (unless otherwise noted, this is defined as persons 65 years and older) is growing rapidly in all industrialized countries, and Canada is no exception. There are two reasons for this.

The first is that, since the end of the 1960s, the birth rate in industrialized countries has been declining and life expectancy has been steadily increasing. The reasons for this go back to the period immediately following World War II. Canadians married in larger numbers as economic prosperity increased during the post-war years. They also had more children, and they had children sooner after marriage than their parents. This resulted in higher fertility, popularly called the baby boom. All this changed after 1966, and Canadian fertility declined. The low birth rate results in a reduction in the number of young persons in the population, and the increased life expectancy results in more people living longer. The Canadian fertility rate has declined from 3.6 children per woman at the height of baby boom in the 1950s to 1.5 children per woman in 2002 (Statistics Canada 22 August 2011). Over this same period, the life expectancy at birth has increased from 66 years to 77 years for males and from 67 to 82 years for females (St-Arnaud, Beaudet, and Tully 2005). This double-edged impact of, on the one hand, the younger population declining due to a decline in the birth rate and, on the other hand, the older population increasing due to an increase in the life expectancy is contributing to the rapid aging of the Canadian population.

The second reason for the rapid aging of the Canadian population is changes in immigration patterns. Immigration waves in the first half of the 20th century were relatively large and consisted mainly of young adults. This earlier immigrant population has aged or died and more recent immigration waves have been smaller and older in age structure.

As a result of these demographic changes, Canada's elderly population has increased rapidly in the 20th and early 21st century. A Statistics Canada (2007b) portrait of seniors revealed that in 1901, 1 in every 20 Canadians was elderly, whereas just over a century later in 2009, 1 in every 8 was elderly. The report predicts that by 2036, when the baby boom generation will have retired, 1 in 4 Canadians will be elderly. Canada's population increased from five million at the beginning of the 20th century to 31.6 million in 2006. Over this same time period, the elderly population grew from merely 271,000 to about 4 million (Statistics Canada 2007b). In other words, the elderly population has grown two and a half times faster than the total population. The proportion of the elderly has recently started to increase even more rapidly because the oldest baby boomers started reaching retirement age in 2011.

Not only that—the elderly population is also growing older. Canada has one million elderly who are over 80 years old, and their number is growing by 42 percent per decade (Statistics Canada 16 July 2002). The result of this increase in longevity among the elderly is that an increasing number of the elderly have elderly parents who are still living. Retired elderly looking after their parents is becoming an increasingly common phenomenon and will become even more widespread as the baby boom generation starts to collect old age security cheques. Both the federal and the provincial governments in Canada have pension and income supplement plans for the elderly. These plans are primarily responsible for reducing poverty among the elderly in Canada. A detailed description of the federal plans can be found on the website of Human Resources and Skills Development Canada (http://www.sdc.gc.ca). Provincial websites also give detailed descriptions of their own programs.

In this scenario of an aging population, the social, economic, and physical well-being of the elderly will continue to be a major issue in Canada. Poverty among the elderly is not only an economic issue for those elderly people themselves, it is also an economic issue—one with huge implications—for the health care system. The following are some of the pertinent questions that we will consider in this chapter: What are the demographic characteristics of the Canadian elderly? What are the sources of their incomes? What are the trends of their poverty?

Characteristics of the Elderly

To understand poverty among the elderly in Canada, we need to understand the demographic, social, and economic characteristics of the elderly population.

Marital status

Marital status of the elderly is an important factor in the study of their poverty. Widowhood affects elderly women's income adversely. An elderly woman without an employer's pension is left with a reduced income after the death of her spouse. Women tend to marry men who are on average two years older than themselves, and they also tend to live on average five years longer than their husbands. This means that a widow who does not remarry will, on average, live as a single person for seven years during her old age. A single elderly woman who lacks a husband's income and did not work when she was younger is unlikely to have a contributory pension. She therefore will be at risk of falling into poverty.

Living arrangements

Elderly women are more likely to be single and in the absence of a spousal pension are more likely to live in poverty than elderly men, who are more likely to live with spouses due to their lower life expectancy. Family and household settings of seniors have also been evolving quickly. Many seniors in Canada live with their spouses or partners. This decreases with age of the elderly for both men and women (Statistics Canada 2004a). Men are far more likely than women to spend their senior years with a spouse or a partner—77 percent of elderly men and only 45 percent of elderly women lived with a spouse or partner in 2001. The likelihood of living with a spouse or partner declines as the elderly age—after age 85, only 13 percent of women and about 59 percent of men lived with a spouse or partner (Statistics Canada 2007b).

Apart from living with a spouse or partner, three other types of common living arrangements among the elderly are:

1. living with at least one of their adult children;
2. living alone; and
3. living in health care institutions.

In 2001, 13 percent of elderly men and 12 percent of elderly women lived in the same household as their children, 16 percent of elderly men and 35 percent of elderly women lived alone, and about 5 percent of elderly men and about 9 percent of elderly women lived in health care institutions (Statistics Canada October 2002).

Living alone is more common even for the elderly aged 85 years and over—23 percent of men and 38 percent of women lived alone in 2001. Living in health care institutions is most common for this group of seniors—23 percent of men and 35 percent of women lived in these institutions. Because the proportion of the elderly continues to increase as the population ages, the absolute numbers of elderly living in institutions will increase.

Old age dependency

Because children and most of the elderly are not members of the labour force, they are considered dependent on the working-age population. In Canada, the elderly usually retire at age 65. Therefore, a ratio of the elderly population (age 65 years and older) to the working-age population (age 15 to 64) is termed *the old age dependency ratio*. This ratio is rapidly increasing in Canada because the elderly population is growing faster than the working-age population. A rise in the old age dependency ratio is an indication of the increasing financial burden on society due to aging. It seems from Statistics Canada's (2007b) population projections that the elderly may overwhelm the Canadian pension system, health care, and social services in the 21st century as the baby boom generation starts retiring. Though this doomsday scenario has some elements of truth, a closer look at the statistics shows that it is overstated.

The proportion of elderly will decline gradually starting in 2036, when the baby boom generation starts to recede. Statistics Canada's (2007b) projections, however, show a steady increase in numbers of elderly until 2056 due to improvement in life expectancy. So it may not be until the middle of the century or later that the old age homes built for the baby boom elderly will become surplus to requirements. The increase in the elderly population in the coming years will put pressure on old age benefits and, hence, on the finances of the elderly.

Education

The 1981 census reported that adults aged 65 and over were less likely to have higher education than adults aged 25 to 64 years. About 50 percent of the elderly reported fewer than nine years of education, compared with only 21 percent of younger adults. The proportion of the elderly with lower levels of education increases with an increase in age. The percentage of the elderly with less than nine years of education was 48 percent in the 65–74 age group, 58 percent in the 75–84 age group, and 61 percent in the 85 and over age group.

What is important here is that the risk of poverty tends to decrease as people have more education. Because education levels increased over generations, there should be a decrease in the number of Canadians who will retire poor in the future.

The Elderly and Poverty

The elderly poor are different from working-age poor. Wedderburn (1970) notes the following four key distinctions between them:

1. there is a difference in the interpretation of poverty;
2. the effect of retirement is unique;
3. there is a myth of homogeneity among the elderly; and
4. the benefits of old age are also unique.

We need to understand these distinguishing features to fully appreciate elderly poverty.

Interpreting elderly poverty

Income as a measure of elderly poverty creates a conceptual problem because the elderly have savings and accumulated assets from their working years, and those elderly who live with their relatives get financial help from them. It can be argued that we should use financial resources rather than income as an indicator of poverty among the elderly. However, there is a high correlation between income and asset ownership, and those who own large assets usually have incomes above the poverty line. This high correlation between asset ownership and income justifies use of income as a measure of poverty among the elderly. The fact that low-income persons are more likely to have low stocks of household items further justifies the use of income as an indicator of poverty (Wedderburn 1970), as does the fact that data on income is much more readily available than data on asset accumulation (e.g., it is difficult to assess the stock of durable goods and clothing in a population).

The financial needs of most elderly persons are less than those of younger people because the elderly enter a period of low income in possession of such assets as a home and household goods that they have accumulated during their working years. Therefore, the income-based poverty line should be set lower for the elderly.

Living arrangements and gender must also be considered in the evaluation of standard of living. Many elderly live with their relatives and are likely to have different needs than those who live on their own. Within that general pattern, however, the living arrangements of elderly men and elderly women differ considerably. In Canada, 61 percent of elderly men live with their own families, compared with 35 percent of elderly women (Statistics Canada 2004a). Elderly women are more likely than elderly men to live alone, and they are also more likely to live in such collective dwellings as hospitals, old age homes, hostels, and rooming houses.

The living arrangements of seniors affect their quality of life—whether they live alone, with a spouse, with a family member, or in an institution. Statistically speaking, whether an elderly person will live alone or not depends on age. In 2006, one-third of the elderly in Canada lived alone (Statistics Canada 2007b). Aging for the elderly often brings widowhood and ill health or infirmity, which are the conditions that lead to living alone and entering an institution or hospital, respectively. The growing number of elderly people living alone has serious economic and social implications for expenditure on health care and social services. Living in institutions is more expensive than living with family and as elaborated later, living alone could bring problems of isolation and loneliness for the elderly. A growing number of widowed and single elderly would prefer to live on their own rather than living with relatives or in institutions (Myles 2012). Improvements in income, subsidies, and services have helped many elderly to live in the community. Though traditional living arrangements—living with relatives or children—is quite common for the Canadian elderly, as mentioned earlier, living alone is becoming common even among older seniors. In 1981, 1 in 5 older seniors (aged 85 years and over) were living alone. By 2001, that had increased to 1 in 3 (Statistics Canada 2007). Living with someone else is often a necessity for poor single or widowed women. A significant number of elderly women live with unmarried daughters who themselves are likely to have low incomes (McDonald 2007).

The effect of retirement

In the parlance of economics, the income of an individual is his or her share in the gross national product. If there is no labour to sell, no land to rent, or no capital to invest, then it automatically means there is no income to earn. The vast majority of the population has only its labour to sell. This implies that most members of society depend on their health and stamina to earn an adequate income by supplying their labour. If individuals are unable to work, for example, because of poor health, they risk becoming poor. Retired people who lack an adequate pension are usually poor because they are unable to work, either due to poor health or due to convention that dictates a person should retire at a specific age. The conventional or mandatory age of retirement over time becomes a societal norm.

Aging is a combination of culture and biology. The cultural norms dictate that at a given age, a person is not fit to work and therefore should retire. It is true that to some extent health and stamina deteriorates due to biological changes caused by aging. The influence of the physical inability and the norm of involuntary retirement on the decision of workers to withdraw from the workforce is difficult to assess. In many countries a worker is entitled to a pension at an earlier age than the formal retirement age.

Because most provincial governments and the federal government offer early retirement options to their employees, the median age of retirement in Canada dropped from 62.3 years in 1991–95 to 61.2 years in 2001 (Mérette 2005). The formal pension age does not seem to have a strong influence in forming retirement norms. When the lower age of retirement was offered to the employees, they preferred to retire younger rather than continuing to work till the formal retirement age of 65. This is also evident from provincial data discussed below.

Many human rights advocates support the abolition of mandatory retirement because it discriminates based on age. The Charter of Rights and Freedoms prohibits discrimination based on age. The Charter was used to challenge the validity of compulsory retirement in 1990, but the Supreme Court of Canada upheld the mandatory retirement. The court concluded that the social upheaval would be monumental if compulsory retirement were abolished (*Toronto Star* 7 December 1990). However, since the1990s, both the federal government and five of the provinces—Ontario, Quebec, Manitoba, Alberta, and Prince Edward Island—have abolished mandatory retirement for their employees. Between the period 1991–95 and the year 2001, the median age of retirement declined from 61.1 to 59.9 in Quebec, from 62.2 to 61.3 in Manitoba, from 62.3 to 60.8 in Prince Edward Island, and from 62.3 to 61.4 in Ontario (Mérette 2005). If workers in these provinces had continued to work to age 65, the impact of cultural norms would have been proven beyond doubt because then one could say that in spite of early retirement option, the workers continued to work to age 65 due to a strong societal norm which prescribed retirement at age 65.

The transition from work to retirement involves financial changes. In the 2002 General Social Survey, one-third of recent retirees reported that their financial situation had worsened after retirement (Statistics Canada 2007b). Involuntary retirees (those who did not want to retire) were more likely to report worsened financial situation after the retirement. The survey also reported that one-third of involuntary retirees in Canada left the labour force because of health problems. That means that the remaining two-thirds retired due to other reasons, including the norm of compulsory retirement at a specific age.

It seems that retirement in old age is partly precipitated by physical changes and partly by individual choice. The individual choice in turn is influenced by societal values, which legitimize retirement from work at a particular age. The interplay between cultural elements and physical changes is quite complex. In essence, whatever the reason for retirement, it leads to permanent withdrawal of a person from the labour force and, in the absence of an adequate income replacement plan, it can lead to poverty.

Old age benefits and poverty

A variety of social security programs provide retirement income for the elderly in Canada. A contributory system also operates apart from federal and provincial government assistance plans in Canada. These programs are geared to perform two main functions—first, to assure the elderly a minimum income to enable them to live in dignity, irrespective of their circumstances during their working years, and, second, to maintain a balance between income before and after the retirement so that the elderly do not experience a drastic reduction in their standard of living (National Council of Welfare April 1984). These programs are meant to fulfil the antipoverty and income replacement goals of a pension system. Poverty among the elderly becomes a possibility only if the elderly are outside of these programs or the amount of retirement pension offered by these programs is below the poverty line.

Heterogeneity among the elderly

Most old age security programs for the elderly assume that they are a homogeneous group, without taking into account differences in gender, race, and ethnicity. In fact, the only feature that all elderly people have in common is their age. Even within the same age group, the elderly may have quite different health and economic conditions. It is a simple fact that a person's economic condition in old age is related to the economic position during that person's working life. We know that every society is economically stratified because people perform different roles during their working years and earn different incomes and, hence, accumulate different levels of assets. The lifestyles of the elderly and their values would have been shaped by their experiences during their working lives, which for most of the elderly in Canada were not spent in poverty. This heterogeneity among the elderly requires that we study their poverty case by case rather than as a group.

The Canadian Elderly in Poverty

Retirement from the labour force can make low income and poverty a long-term feature for the elderly. The special feature of poverty among the elderly is that once the aged become poor, there is little expectation that they will move out of that condition on their own for the rest of their life. In 2002, among more than half a million poor elderly, 77 percent were unattached and 23 percent lived in families (Table 3-1). Poverty among the elderly is largely a problem of the unattached elderly. The rate of poverty is almost eight times greater for the unattached elderly than the elderly in families, and the rate of poverty among the elderly in families was almost half that of the non-elderly. However, the unattached elderly had higher rates of poverty than their non-elderly counterparts.

Table 3-1   Percent Distribution of Poor by Age, Sex, and Family Type, Canada 2002

	Elderly		Non-Elderly (aged 18–64)	
	Percent	Number	Percent	Number
Economic Families				
Female head	5.1	66,000	10.8	949,000
Male head	4.7	63,000	8.5	714,000
Total	**4.9**	**129,000**	**9.7**	**1,663,000**
Unattached Individuals				
Female	41.5	341,000	32.2	439,000
Male	31.0	92,000	27.7	487,000
Total	**38.7**	**433,000**	**30.9**	**926,000**

Source: Statistics Canada. 2005. CANSIM Table 202-0802. Statistics Canada Catalogue no. 75-202-XIE. Ottawa: Statistics Canada.

Poverty rates among Canadian elderly have declined between 1983 and 2002 (Table 3-2). This reduction has benefited elderly men as well as elderly women. Consequently, the poverty gap between elderly men and elderly women has narrowed. Though poverty rates among both unattached elderly men and unattached elderly women have declined, the poverty rate for unattached elderly women remains almost eight times higher than that for elderly women in families (Table 3-2). The poverty rate of unattached elderly men is six times higher than that of elderly men in families. It seems that the difference in earnings between women and men carries over into retirement because pension benefits are based on their earnings during younger ages (National Council of Welfare 2004). Because women, on average, live longer than men, they are more likely to deplete their savings during their lifetime.

Table 3-2   Trends in Poverty Rates among Elderly by Family Type, Canada, Selected Years

	Family Head			Unattached		
	Female	Male	Total	Women	Men	Total
1983	12.5	14.7	13.7	71.6	57.0	68.1
1991	8.0	7.7	7.8	54.5	42.0	51.4
2002	5.1	4.7	4.9	41.5	31.0	38.7

Source: Statistics Canada. 2005. CANSIM Table 202-0802. Statistics Canada Catalogue no. 75-202-XIE. Ottawa: Statistics Canada.

The difference in the poverty rate between the elderly in families and unattached elderly is simply due to the fact that the elderly in families benefit from the pooled income of two persons.

Income of the elderly

The incomes of the poor elderly in Canada were not only lower than those of the non-elderly, they were often thousands of dollars below the poverty line (Statistics Canada's low income cut-off). The average income reported by poor elderly couples in one-earner households in the 2001 census was $17,913; that of poor unattached elderly, $13,346. This was only 38 percent of the incomes of their respective non-poor elderly counterparts (National Council of Welfare 2004). The average income of poor unattached elderly women, $14,010, represents 47 percent of that of unattached non-poor elderly women. Though not all elderly in Canada live in poverty, a large number of them are concentrated on the lower rungs of the income ladder. According to Statistics Canada (2011b), the median market income of the elderly in families is 43 percent of the median market income of the non-elderly in families; for the unattached elderly, this ratio is 57 percent for men and 49 percent women. A large proportion of the elderly poor are women because the majority of them were homemakers during their younger years and did not have employers' pensions to rely on.

Sources of income

The reduction in poverty among the elderly since the 1980s in Canada is a success story. To understand why the Canadian elderly have modest incomes and why a sizeable number of them still live under conditions of poverty in spite of two decades of decline, we must investigate their sources of income.

The government income transfer plans, such as federal Old Age Security (OAS), Guaranteed Income Supplement (GIS), and Canada/Quebec Pension Plan (C/QPP) are the major sources of income for the elderly in Canada. These public sector plans provide 96 percent of the total income of elderly couples, 75 percent for unattached elderly women, and 82 percent for unattached elderly men (Table 3-3). The remaining 4 percent, 25 percent, and 18 percent, respectively, comes from private and other sources (Table 3-3).

Employment opportunities are quite rare for people 65 and older. Only 14 percent of elderly men and 9 percent of elderly women were in the labour force in 2009, and many of them had part-time or seasonal jobs—often, their age precluded any full-time work (National Seniors Council

Table 3-3   Income for Poor Elderly by Source and Family Status, Canada 2001

Source	Couples (%)	Unattached Women (%)	Unattached Men (%)
Public Sources			
Old Age Security (OAS)	36	27	29
Guaranteed Income Supplement (GIS) and Spousal Allowance	28	23	25
Canada and Quebec Pension Plan (C/QPP)	30	23	26
GST/HST credits and supplements	2	2	2
Total public	96	75	82
Private Sources			
Private pension	–	15	9
Investments	–	8	7
Total private	–	23	16
Other	4	2	2
Total	**100**	**100**	**100**

Source: Adapted from National Council of Welfare. 2004. *Poverty Profile 2001*. Ottawa: National Council of Welfare. Tables 6.1 and 6.3.

2009). It is clear that advancing age is an impediment to an employment income for the elderly.

Today most of the elderly remain dependent on government for their income because most elderly men of today worked with employers who did not provide pension plans for their employees and most elderly women of today stayed at home during their working-age years. More than 90 percent of the income of the poor elderly in 2001 came from government transfer programs (National Council of Welfare 2004). It is clear then that the improvement in the government plans for the elderly after the 1980s is the main cause of the decline in poverty among the elderly in Canada.

Income Drop after Retirement

Poverty among the elderly to a large extent is a reflection of their income in their younger years. Most people who are poor or near-poor during their working years remain poor during their old age. At the same time, many middle-income Canadians join the ranks of the poor or the near-poor when their income drops after retirement. The elderly who face poverty after their retirement, on average, had income almost double the poverty line before retirement (National Council of Welfare February 1984). This makes government programs such as Old Age Security (OAS), Guaranteed Income Supplement (GIS), and Canada/Quebec Pension Plan (C/QPP) crucial in reducing and also preventing poverty among the elderly. Improvement in these income sources has been the major cause of reduction of poverty among Canadian elderly since the 1980s. Many poor elderly in Canada had middle-class incomes in their working years. The National Council of Welfare reported in 1984 and 1989 that the half of the elderly who received OAS also received GIS and that one-quarter of those who received GIS qualified for the maximum amount because their only source of income was the OAS allowance. In 2006, 35 percent of the elderly who received OAS also received GIS (Statistics Canada 22 July 2009). The GIS is an allowance that supplements the incomes of lower-income pensioners. This decline in GIS recipients is a testimony of improvement of incomes of seniors in Canada. The importance of private pensions and Registered Retirement Savings Plans (RRSPs) as sources of income, especially for women, has grown significantly in the recent years. Private retirement savings in 2005 represented about 38 percent of elderly men's income and 27 percent of elderly women's income (National Seniors Council 2009). This is an increase from 23 percent for men and 16 percent for women in 2001.

Although in 2007 families headed by the elderly had incomes that were only 46 percent of those of non-elderly families, the incomes of elderly families have been rising faster than those of non-elderly Canadians. The average income of elderly families grew by 36 percent between 1998 and 2007, compared with 18 percent for families headed by non-elderly persons (Statistics Canada 3 June 2009).

Because proportionately more unattached individuals are poor as a whole, the change in the average income of elderly and non-elderly unattached individuals from 1998 to 2007 is not significantly different. Unattached elderly men earned 56 percent of the average income of unattached non-elderly men, and unattached elderly women earned 47 percent of the average income of unattached non-elderly women (Statistics Canada 3 June 2009). Though the gap between the average income of the elderly and of non-elderly families is narrowing, elderly families still earn less than half as much as non-elderly families because income drops significantly after retirement. And that drop in income after retirement brings some of the elderly below the poverty line.

The effect of the drop in income after retirement becomes severe if aging also brings disability. The following story from an elderly woman living in the Kitchener–Waterloo region of Ontario reveals what happens to seniors when their income drops after retirement.

I am 67 years old and my husband is 76. About 8 years ago, my husband's health began to deteriorate and he was diagnosed with Parkinson's disease . . . and Alzheimer's. . . . All of my husband's Old Age Security, Guaranteed Income Supplement and Canada Pension is supposed to be turned over to the nursing home but I need to hold back some of his pension money in order to live. I collect OAS and GIS also but it's very little and, after I've paid the rent, I'm left with less than $400.00 per month for food, utilities, transportation, clothing, personal, and medical needs. When my husband was still at home, our combined pensions were enough for our needs but now we're basically maintaining two residences on the same income (Social Planning Council of Kitchener–Waterloo 2000, 3).

Income Inequality and the Elderly

According to a study conducted by Health and Welfare Canada published in 1979, retirement income appears to reflect and reinforce the income inequalities of the working years. A report by the National Council of Welfare published five years later (February 1984) found this conclusion to be still valid. But things changed in the 1990s. The "maturation" of the Canada and Quebec Pension Plans (C/QPP) has been one factor contributing to the rising incomes of seniors. Between 1980 and 2003, the share of elderly men receiving income from C/QPP increased from 68.6 percent to 95.8 percent, and the share of elderly women receiving income from C/QPP increased from 34.8 percent to 85.8 percent (Statistics Canada 2007b). A large change in C/QPP female recipients is a result of the rise in their workforce participation rate. This is part of Canada's success story of alleviating poverty among its seniors.

Though poverty among the Canadian elderly has declined, low income among the recent immigrant elderly is a concern. According to Statistics Canada (2007b), in 2001, among immigrant seniors with 20 years or less of Canadian residency, about 17 percent of those in family households and 67 percent of unattached individuals had incomes below the poverty line. These rates are even higher than those for the Aboriginal elderly. In that same year, 13 percent of Aboriginal seniors in the family households and about 50 percent of unattached Aboriginal seniors reported low income (Statistics Canada 2007b).

There are several reasons for higher poverty rates among recent immigrant seniors. As we have seen in Chapter 2, on ethnic poverty, a higher proportion of recent immigrants live in poverty in Canada. A person who has lived in Canada less than 20 years is unlikely to have accumulated enough working years to earn a decent employer's pension or a contributory pension from Canada/Quebec Pension Plan (C/QPP). It is also possible that some immigrants who sponsored their parents are unable to support them due to their own low incomes.

Non-monetary considerations for poverty among the elderly

The elderly do not live by money alone. Many of them own homes and enjoy services and subsidies that are not reflected by analyses based on income data. As far back as 1979, Stone and MacLean (1979) calculated that the total income of the elderly would be 30 percent higher if the value of non-monetary sources of income and unreported cash gifts were taken into account. As revealed in the next section, home ownership remains high among the elderly and the value of non-monetary sources of the elderly still may be considerable. Most elderly do not participate in the labour force and therefore do not contribute to pension plans, unemployment insurance, union dues, commuting costs, and other employment-related expenses. The elderly also face a lower tax bite from Revenue Canada than do non-elderly taxpayers, partly because of lower incomes and partly because of special tax concessions, such as the age exemption. These benefits increase the net income of the elderly.

Many elderly who own their own home are denied social assistance and legal aid because in most jurisdictions in Canada home ownership is considered in calculating eligibility for social assistance and legal aid. As we will see in the next section, for the elderly, equating home ownership to financial security is a myth that needs to be dispelled.

"House Rich and Cash Poor" Elderly

A large majority of the elderly own their own home. According to the National Seniors Council (2009), although 70 percent of all seniors own their home, two-thirds of low-income elderly are renters. The important feature of the elderly home ownership is that about 90 percent of the elderly had paid off their mortgages (Statistics Canada 23 July 2004). As a result, shelter costs of the elderly tend to be lower than those of persons under the age of 65. But that advantage is offset by the fact that the average income of the elderly is also lower than that of non-elderly persons.

Comparisons between poor and non-poor elderly people in terms of home ownership are quite revealing. Even among low-income elderly family heads in 1981 who were homeowners, most had paid off their mortgage, and thus needed less income than the average Canadian, who makes rent or mortgage payments every month (National Council of Welfare, February 1984). However, elderly homeowners continue to incur expenses on running their owned dwelling in spite of their limited income. Property taxes, utilities (heat, electricity, and water), insurance, maintenance, and repairs put a strain on their modest incomes. Consumer price index figures (Statistics Canada June 2005) show that the price of energy went up by 44 percent between 1995 and 2005. The cost of maintaining a household rose by 61 percent, and repair costs increased by 13 percent over these 10 years. These expenses formed a larger proportion of the modest incomes of the elderly compared with their non-elderly counterparts. The spending differences on basic necessities—food, shelter, clothing, household operations, medical and health care, and transportation—are still substantial considering the modest incomes of a large majority of the elderly.

Because of these anomalies, some elderly are what we call "house rich and cash poor." In other words, home ownership removes a significant amount of their modest incomes because of operating costs. Their homes are older than average, advancing age forbids them to make repairs themselves, and, therefore, the costly expenses required to replace a worn roof or faulty plumbing are particularly worrisome to the elderly poor.

You may be asking yourself, why don't elderly homeowners simply sell their homes and trade their principal asset for cash? The problem with that scenario is that even if they sell, they need to find affordable alternative accommodation—a rarity in many Canadian cities. Moreover, this will be only a short-term solution and may not leave them any better off in the long run. As mentioned earlier, the elderly tend to own older homes, which usually fetch a lower price than the newer homes owned by the non-elderly. So while the "cash poor" part of the expression holds, the "house rich" part is an exaggeration.

In conclusion, we can say that the incomes of elderly Canadians have improved since the 1980s and that elderly people in the future are less likely to be poor than their contemporary counterparts because of improved education levels. However, the unattached elderly, particularly women, still remain at high risk of poverty.

Conceptual Explanations

There are many factors related to elderly poverty, including pension plans, norms governing retirement age, health, and living arrangements of the elderly. Poverty in old age is also linked to employers' pension plans available to workers and government social security programs available to the elderly. Employers' pension is an indicator of income of future elderly, and incomes from government social security programs are a determinant of poverty among the current elderly. We saw earlier that compulsory retirement is partly a cultural phenomenon, because societal norms decide at what age its members should retire, and partly a biological phenomenon, because in many instances a worker has to retire due to health problems caused by aging. So conceptually, poverty among elderly is complex. It is interplay between pension plans, government benefits, biology, and cultural norms. Living arrangements of the elderly in various societies also have cultural bearings. For example, in many eastern societies, elderly parents are expected to live with their children and children are expected to support their elderly parents. But there is no distinct culture of the elderly to form a culture of poverty. The elderly come from different cultural backgrounds and they pursued diverse occupations in their younger years, when their values and norms were shaped; they are, therefore, unlikely to form a homogenous culture. The culture of poverty explanation will not be helpful to explain poverty among a culturally diverse group.

The situational perspective may explain certain aspects of elderly poverty. Aging, the availability of employers' pension plans, and the efficacy of government social security programs are the situational factors that affect poverty among the elderly. Poverty can be ameliorated by lessening the burden of aging with subsidized or free health care programs. Employers can be given incentives to provide contributory pension plans to their workers so that their incomes during retirement will not fall below the poverty line, and government social security programs can augment inadequate employers' pensions. Canada has done quite well in providing universal health care, drug plans, contributory pension plans, a universal old age security program, a guaranteed minimum income, and spousal allowances to its elderly. These programs have helped to reduce poverty among the elderly.

Stigma and exclusion are important aspects of poverty in old age. In youth-oriented Western societies there is a stigma associated with old age, and employers are reluctant to hire older workers, particularly retirees who need to work to supplement their benefits. Though several provinces in Canada have lifted the mandatory retirement age, older workers do face a difficult time finding work (Statistics Canada 2007b).

Living arrangements of the elderly are an important predictor of their isolation. In 2001, more than 7 percent of the elderly lived in institutions and about 27 percent of them lived alone. The main reasons of social isolation of the elderly are:

- living alone;
- widowhood;
- loss of social role due to loss of employment; and
- health problems.

Studies show that seniors living below the poverty line suffer from social isolation. For example, one-third of the poor elderly living alone saw neither friends nor neighbours for as much as two weeks at a time, and one-fifth did not have any phone conversations with friends or family (Klinenberg 2002; Walker and Herbitter 2005). Social isolation of the poor elderly and especially of the poor unattached elderly increases the risk of health and mental problems. Social exclusion of the elderly is likely to make living harder for the elderly living in poverty. Therefore, seeking solutions to elderly poverty in the light of social exclusion also makes sense.

Chapter 4

Women in Poverty

Introduction

The profile of poverty in Canada changed dramatically starting in the 1980s. Today, poor women outnumber poor men and they run a higher risk of poverty than men. This phenomenon has been termed as the *feminization of poverty*. The 2009 downturn in the labour market affected women less than men. Male-dominated industries such as manufacturing, construction, and natural resources were the hardest hit by employment losses. In contrast, employment continued to grow in female-dominated service sectors such as health care, social assistance, educational services, finance, and insurance (Ferrao 1 April 2011). While unemployment rate among women did rise, from 5.7 percent in 2008 to 7.0 percent in 2009, the increase was steeper for men, from 6.7 percent in 2008 to 9.4 percent in 2009, which is the highest rate observed since 1996, the end of the 1990s slowdown (Ferrao 1 April 2011). This change in unemployment rates has contributed to the decline in poverty among working age women and, hence, reversed the trend in the feminization of poverty among these women. If the 2008–2009 recession pattern of higher unemployment among men continues in the future, the feminization of poverty may be replaced by a new term, *masculinization of poverty*.

According to Statistics Canada (2004b) almost 36 percent of the more than one million female lone parents in Canada lived below the poverty line (low income cut-off). Statistics Canada defines a lone-parent family as a family headed by an adult who is single, separated, divorced, or widowed. Most poor single mothers are unable to join the labour force due to a lack of subsidized daycare services for their children. This inaccessibility of the labour market, together with the way we socialize girls and the persistence of inequalities in the institution of marriage, are the main reasons for women's poverty. The following sections of this chapter provide a demographic profile of lone-parent families and discuss changes in the feminization of poverty and consequences of poverty for women.

Demographic Profile of Lone-Parent Families

The vast majority of lone-parent families in Canada are headed by women. Female lone-parent families are poor because they lack the man's earnings, and the mother's earning power is diminished by her inability to work due to her children's need for her care. To understand the changing profile of poverty among women, it is necessary to examine the changes in lone-parent families in Canada.

Canadian censuses reveal that prior to 1966, husband-and-wife families increased and lone-parent families decreased because improvements in life expectancy resulted in more women surviving and more parents living together until the "empty nest stage" (i.e., the children leaving home). Economic prosperity after World War II resulted in a baby boom. All this changed after 1966. Canadian fertility declined, and lone-parent families experienced higher growth than two-parent families. Between the 1966 census and the 1981 census, the proportion of lone-parent families increased by 92 percent whereas husband-and-wife families increased only by 40 percent (Miron 1988). Between the 1981 and the 2006 censuses the proportion of lone-parent families increased by 55 percent, whereas the husband-and-wife families declined by 28 percent (Statistics Canada 2007a).

Marital status

There was a rapid increase in divorced lone parents in Canada after the 1968 amendments to the Divorce Act. The amendments permitted easier and faster divorce for petitioners. Prior to 1968, the only ground for divorce was adultery (Pike 1975), except in Nova Scotia, which also included cruelty. The 1968 Act extended the grounds for divorce to cruelty, bigamy, various unnatural sexual acts, long-term imprisonment, alcoholism, drug addiction, and long-term unwillingness or inability to consummate marriage. The number of divorces in Canada increased from 11,300 in 1968 to 29,900 in 1971, to 70,400 in 1982. The number declined slightly, to 68,600, in 1983. After the advent of a new "no-fault" divorce law in 1987, it peaked at 92,200. In 2003, it had stabilized at around 70,000 (Statistics Canada 2006b). The income of women declines sharply after divorce, and the lack of legal protection from alimony evaders puts many of them in precarious economic circumstances, leading to a life of long-term poverty. The probability of remarriage is much lower for lone mothers, who usually obtain custody of children after divorce. Only 53 percent of women compared with 70 percent of men remarry after divorce (Statistics Canada 1990).

The proportion of separated or divorced women among female lone parents in Canada decreased from 51.6 percent in 1981 to 48.6 percent in 2001; this decline was offset by an increase in the share of never-married female lone parents from 11.1 percent to 28.5 percent (Statistics Canada 2006b). Dissolution of union by death also leaves a disproportionately larger number of women without spouses. In 2001 among Canadian elderly, 221,000 women and 43,000 men were widowed lone parents (Statistics Canada 2006b). This meant that more than 80 percent of widowed lone parents were women. The life expectancy of women increased at a higher rate than that of men. The proportion of widows is likely to rise because women live longer and are usually on average two years younger than their husbands at the time of marriage. The dissolution of marital union due to the death of the husband deprives a woman of the man's income or pension.

There has also been a marked increase in never-married mothers. Births to unmarried mothers have shown a rising trend since the availability of data, which goes back to 1921 in Canada (Sharma 1982a). The rise in out-of-wedlock births, in spite of the availability of a large variety of contraceptives, suggests a change in societal attitude and wider acceptance of having a child without being married. Not only have births to single mothers steadily increased, but also a more liberated lifestyle and living arrangements that emerged in the 1960s encouraged increasing numbers of never-married mothers to choose to keep and rear their children. When an unmarried young woman has a child, this usually leads to her dropping out of school, which in turn results in lifelong low income due to a low level of education.

The incidence of poverty varies greatly by the family status of women. For example, in Ontario today, sole-support parents make up 31 percent of social assistance cases. Of those sole-support parents, 93 percent are women (Commission for the Review of Social Assistance in Ontario 2011). As was noted above, fatherless families are poor because they lack the man's earnings and the mother's earning power is diminished by her children's need for her care.

Living arrangements of lone-parent families

According to the National Council of Welfare (1990), almost 73 percent of lone mothers were maintainers of their households and were living without other persons (other than their children) as part of their households. This means that a large number of single mothers do not have the advantage of having related or unrelated persons sharing in the household expenses. It also means that a large number of them do not have a person around to help them to care for and rear their children. In the absence of adequate daycare and help of relatives, this makes it difficult for lone mothers to earn their living away from home, as children in their formative years require their mothers for care and mothers require assurance that their children are in good hands.

Housing

As compared with husband-and-wife families, lone-parent families are at a disadvantage regarding tenure, conditions of dwelling, and ability to afford a dwelling. Lone parents have a much lower rate of home ownership as compared with husband-and-wife families with children. According to the 2006 census, one-third of houses of female lone parents needed major repair. Female lone-parent families who rented their dwellings were in a still more difficult situation. They had half the average income of those who owned a dwelling, yet half of them spent more than 35 percent of their income on shelter and one-third of them even spent 50 percent or more of their income on housing.

The Feminization of Poverty

Two reports were of great significance for the study of poverty in Canada. The Royal Commission on the Status of Women (1970) reported poverty among women as an unexpectedly significant finding. The Special Senate Committee on Poverty (1971) dismissed it in a four-page chapter entitled "The poor mother and child day care centres." Because the Senate Committee on Poverty was seen as not living up to its mandate by some poverty activists, *The Real Poverty Report* by Adam, Cameron, Hill, and Penz (1971) was written to be a final report. Unfortunately, this report also did not see it appropriate to give adequate attention to millions of Canadian women in poverty.

From the time of these earlier studies until today, anyone whose own income or whose family's income is below the poverty line has been considered poor. Unfortunately, this definition does not encompass all economically deprived women. It assumes that women living in the same household have equal access to the family's resources and that there are no middle- and upper-class husbands who fail to provide their wives with the basic necessities. This definition also unfairly excludes those poor women who happened to live with a well-off relative out of necessity rather than by choice. However, despite these definitional limitations, statistics on women in poverty are quite stark. In 2005, of about 1.8 million poor women, two-thirds lived in families and one-third were unattached (Statistics Canada 2006b). Whether poor women lived in families or whether they were unattached, their poverty percentage was higher than that of poor men, thus confirming the "feminization of poverty" phenomenon. Also, women's earnings in Canada have been on average around 60 percent of men's earnings since 1990 (Statistics Canada 2006b). In other words, women run a higher risk of poverty than men and they make up a larger percentage of the poor.

The feminization of poverty is particularly valid for elderly women and women in economic families. The poverty rate of elderly women in 1990 was about 114 percent higher than that of the elderly men; in 2009, it was still 97 percent higher (Table 4-1). The poverty rate of women in the economic families in 1990 was about 26 percent higher than that of men; in 2009, it was about 10 percent higher (Table 4-1). Among working-age women in economic families, the poverty rate was about 48 percent higher than for their male counterparts in 1990 and 19 percent higher in 2009.

Table 4-1 Persons Below Low Income Cut-Offs (after tax), Canada, 1990 and 2009

	Percent		Female to Male Ratio (%)	
	1990	2009	1990	2009
Among All Persons				
Male	10.4	9.5		
Female	13.2	9.6	29.9	1.1
Working-Age Persons (18–64)				
Male	9.9	10.6		
Female	12.4	10.4	25.3	-1.9
Elderly (65 and over)				
Male	5.9	3.4		
Female	14.4	6.7	114.1	97.1
Among Persons in Economic Families				
Male	8.0	6.2		
Female	10.1	6.8	26.3	9.7
Working-Age Persons (18–64)				
Male	6.2	5.8		
Female	9.2	6.9	48.4	19.0
Unattached Individuals				
Male	28.2	27.4		
Female	34.2	25.9	21.3	-5.5

Source: Statistics Canada. June 2011a. "CANSIM Table 202-0802." *Persons in Low Income after Tax.* Statistics Canada Catalogue no. 75-202-X. Ottawa: Statistics Canada. Last modified 15 June 2011.

Table 4-2   Number and Percentage of Persons in Low Income by Gender and Family Status, 2005

	Number (000s)	Percent
All persons	**3,409**	**100.0**
Males	1,637	48.0
Females	1,772	52.0
Persons in Economic Families	**2,021**	**100.0**
Males	950	47.0
Females	1,071	53.0
Unattached Individuals	**1,388**	**100.0**
Males	687	49.5
Females	701	50.5

Source: Statistics Canada. 2005. "Table 11.1." *Income in Canada 2005*. Statistics Canada Catalogue no. 75-202-XIE. Ottawa: Statistics Canada. Last modified 5 May 2008. Available online.

Another indicator of the "feminization of poverty" is what is known as the proportionality index. This index is calculated by dividing the percentage of low-income women by the percentage of women in all incomes. According to 2006 census, the percentage of women in Canada is 51 percent and a 2005 Statistics Canada report shows that women make up 52 percent of low-income persons (Table 4-2). The proportionality index is thus 1.02, which indicates that women are over-represented among Canada's poor. A remarkable growth in single-parent families is the major reason for the growth in low-income families led by women (National Council of Welfare April 1988). Between 2001 and 2006, lone-parent families grew by 8 percent whereas couple families grew by 4 percent (Statistics Canada 21 November 2008).

Words speak louder than statistics. The following experiences of women representing wives, single mothers, and women living alone are reproduced verbatim to show that the extent of hardship endured by women in poverty remained unchanged over the decades and that poverty is a unique experience for each individual. This first description is from 1978.

Anna F. is 29 years old. She became poor five years ago after the birth of her second child. . . .

From then on, the lack of money became chronic and quarrels were frequent between Anna and her husband. Twice separated, they got back together again. The first time he left, her phone was disconnected, the electricity was cut off for a week, and the living-room furniture was seized for debts. Following reconciliation, Anna had another child. . . .

The worst right now, she says, is the constant worry over bills. The couple has many debts. . . . And although winter is approaching, last year's heating bills are not yet fully paid. (National Council of Welfare 1979)

This description is from 1988. Donna, 22, is married with two children.

We came from Jamaica to join our families here. We thought life would be better in Canada. . . .

My husband is a labourer and I am a machine operator in a clothing factory. . . . The job is O.K.; it's piece-work. . . . by 2:30 pm I can't do much, because I get tired. I'd like a job that is cleaner . . . and I get allergies from the fleece. My husband likes his job. . . . The shift work is difficult though, because he finds it hard to sleep. If he goes to work tired it can be dangerous, because he operates machinery. . . . If we could afford it I'd stay home with our children. . . .

We have no savings, no credit cards. We never take a vacation. . . . We don't own a car or a house. . . . We all do without things, even the kids, and when we say no they cry and we feel bad. When my husband's grandmother died recently in Jamaica he couldn't send any money to help bury her. . . .

We get sad and worry sometimes. My husband fantasizes about running away to escape when he feels overwhelmed. (Social Assistance Review Committee 1988, 287–288)

If you think that living in poverty has become any easier in recent times, think again. Here is a description of what it is like to be poor circa 2002:

A single mother of one child in Ontario receives $957 per month of assistance before deductions. Then she has to spend $675 on rent, $200 on groceries, and has $82 left to pay bills. . . . She has to explain to her son why he can't go on school trips like the other kids, why he is teased for . . . being dressed in old third-hand clothes, why he can't go to a friend's birthday party because there's no money for a . . . gift, why he can't participate in hot dog day at school because it costs money, why the milk tastes different because she's had to water it down, why by the end of the month they have to go down to the food bank. . . . Being poor limits your choices. . . . Managing on a very low income is . . . a 7-day-a-week job . . . no vacation or relief. Poverty grinds you down, body and soul. (Morris 2002)

The census distinguishes between wives of low-income husbands and low-income female family heads. A family is defined as a husband and a wife with or without children, or a single parent with children. In a female single-parent family, the mother is per definition the head of the household, whereas in the case of a husband-and-wife family, it is usually the man who is reported as the head.

Although married women are comparatively less likely to be poor, they make up the largest group among poor women because the vast majority of Canadian women are married. Put another way, a small percentage of poor wives adds up to more poor women than a larger percentage of any other female group. For example in 2001, 295,000 poor couples with children,158,000 poor couples without children, and 58,000 poor elderly couples meant over a quarter million married women in poverty (National Council of Welfare 2004).

The predominant factor responsible for poverty among women under 65 years of age is the presence of children itself. The presence of young children affects the economic status of their mothers because, as was noted earlier, lack of affordable daycare makes it difficult to hold down a job.

The second factor is the influence of the employment status of the husband or the major earner in the family. While more than three-quarters of non-poor husbands are employed full-time year-round, less than one-third of low-income married men are that lucky (National Council of Welfare 1988). In 2001, the poverty rate for families with the major earner working year-round full-time was 4 percent, whereas for families with the major earner working part of the year and part-time it was 46 percent (National Council of Welfare 2004).

The third factor that makes women vulnerable to poverty is their age and being unattached (Statistics Canada June 2011a). There is no doubt that young, never-married mothers with small children are at high risk of poverty. But they are not typical. The typical spouseless mother is 40 to 45 years of age, divorced or separated, and living with teenage children. This typical spouseless mother is less likely to be poor because spouseless mothers are more likely to be poor when they are young. Among single mothers under the age of 35, 2 out of 3 have incomes below the poverty line, compared with 1 out of 3 among older single mothers (National Council of Welfare April 1988). Because older mothers have older children, their entry to the labour force is less likely to be dependent on the availability of child care. And older children are also more likely to support themselves.

The fourth factor responsible for the low-income status of single mothers is that single mothers, particularly young single mothers, tend to have very low levels of education. For an unattached person with only high-school education, the risk of poverty is more than three times higher than for a university-educated unattached person. With only elementary schooling, it is four times higher (National Council of Welfare 2004). A well-paid job is the only insurance a single mother has against poverty. Education is an important determinant of one's income and access to a job.

Poor women living alone

The following are vignettes of women who do not live with spouses or relatives and are elderly or near-elderly. You will see that their plight is not very different from that of the married women you read about above.

The first one, from 67-year-old Mary S., is from 1978.

> If you're really interested, I'll tell you what it's like being an old woman alone who's only got the government pension to live on. . . . It's wearing out your second-hand shoes going from one store to another to find the cheapest cuts of meat. It's hating having to buy toilet tissue or soap or toothpaste because you can't eat it. It's picking the marked down fruits and vegetables from the half-rotting stuff in the back of the stores that used to be given away to farmers to feed their animals. . . .
>
> How do we manage? We pay our rent and utilities and we eat less.
>
> We live in fear. Fear of the future, of more illness. . . . Fear that the cheque won't arrive . . . to pay our rent. Fear that we will run out of food before the next cheque comes in. So, fear holds you in line. (National Council of Welfare 1979)

This description is from 1988.

> Rosa, 64, is a Portuguese woman who arrived in Canada at age 62.
>
> Rosa does not speak much English, so her friends helped Rosa call the welfare office. . . . The welfare office explained that Rosa was not eligible because she was under sponsorship and her son was responsible for her. She was referred to immigration. The immigration office granted Rosa a hearing, which her son would have to attend to prove he could no longer support Rosa. He did not attend because he is too proud to discuss family problems. . . .
>
> Rosa's friend . . . called . . . Toronto Housing to . . . get a subsidized apartment. She was told that because Rosa was still under sponsorship, she would not be eligible. . . .
>
> Rosa knows she cannot return to Portugal because she has sold small house and belongings. She is left in Canada, estranged from her son, with no financial assistance and no housing. (Social Assistance Review Committee 1988)

At 60, Patricia Cummings-Diaz expected more from life. This is from 2011.

> She is currently renting an apartment in North York with a grown son because she cannot afford to live alone. . . . She is . . . among the working poor trying to eke out a living . . . has a university degree, works one day a week as a research assistant . . . with a local group dedicated to helping poor women. Yet she can't make ends meet on a monthly wage of $1,050, plus an additional $250 from the government as widow's allowance. . . . Poverty is a social disease. . . .
> One way to get serious is by adopting a national housing strategy. . . . And, if such a strategy had existed many years ago, when she was a young widowed mother raising three children, she would not have uprooted her children as much, always moving from place to place because the only housing she could afford was in dangerous neighbourhoods. (Teotonio 2011)

Household formation with no relatives by single women has increased in Canada. There are two reasons for this. There is an increased tendency for young women to leave their parents' homes to live alone. And elderly women who were married tend to live alone because they outlive their husbands due to their higher life expectancy. Because the majority of young childless women are students living alone and only a small minority of young childless women are unemployed, the proportion of young childless women in poverty appears to be relatively smaller. However, it is very difficult to estimate the extent of poverty among childless young women because money obtained in the form of student loans and gifts from their parents is not classified as income. Therefore, we do not know for sure how many of them live in financial hardship. According to the National Council of Welfare (April 1988) young female students are just a small proportion of all women living alone. Three-quarters of women who live alone are over the age of 55, and most of them live in poverty. No single factor is sufficient to explain poverty among Canadian women, yet one common element that distinguishes poor women is that they cannot depend on a man's support.

Causes and Consequences of Poverty among Women

As was mentioned above, the common element that distinguishes many poor women from non-poor women is that they lack a man's or partner's earning power. The causes of poverty among women are lodged in many social and economic institutions of society: socialization, marriage, motherhood, marital dissolution, and women's position in labour market.

Socialization

The process of socialization reinforces the inferiority of females and the superiority of males in most societies, and Canada would be no exception. Through socialization, societal values and beliefs are internalized, that is, they are consolidated and embedded as their own values and beliefs when it comes to moral behaviour. Through the process of socialization, girls internalize values that inhibit their capacity to fully compete in a male-dominated economic system. Many values and beliefs that girls internalize when they are young encourage them to enter lower-paying occupations. For example, most women in Canada work in the low-paying services sector.

Despite efforts to promote gender equality through legislation requiring equal pay for equal work, and despite the creation of affirmative action programs, little has changed in the way girls and boys are brought up. What Forisha (1978) pointed out decades ago, that parents' attitudes and expectations vary greatly according to the sex of the child, and generally to the disadvantage of girls, is still true (Canadian Council on Learning 2007). A male infant is defined by adults as "big, tough, active, aggressive and alert" and a female infant as "little, beautiful, pretty, cute, cuddly, passive and delicate" (Forisha 1978, 322).

Psychological studies (e.g., Stewart 1976) indicate that gender differences reinforced by socialization become completely internalized by the time children reach school age. Studies conducted in the 1970s and 1980s are illuminating in that today's poor elderly women were students in the 1970s and today's poor younger women were high-school students in the mid-1980s. In her study set in Ottawa, Russell (1987) demonstrated that the subordinate position of women in society is promoted in the school system. During their high-school years, boys were found to have become more career-conscious, whereas many girls had low career ambitions, were afraid of university, and had already settled on such "female-dominated" occupations as nursing, secretarial, and child care services (Russell 1978). Thus, schools contributed to the social reproduction of class and gender inequalities (Russell 1987). Girls and working-class students had lower aspirations to attend university than did boys and middle-class students (Porter, Porter, and Blishen 1982). More than half of the girls believed that their main role in life was to be a wife and mother (Russell 1978, 1987). There is nothing wrong in these beliefs. However, because most women internalized these beliefs during their socialization, their capacity to compete in the labour market in their adult life was hampered and the risk of poverty increased due to a lack of an employer's pension, especially if women divorced or became widowed.

Marriage and motherhood

Though marriages today in Canada are not arranged as they were in traditional, pre-industrialized societies, women still end up marrying men with backgrounds very similar to their own. Demographic marriage tables tell us that 92 out of every 100 women will get married during their lifetime (Sharma 1987), and in almost all cases, marriage will not be a social and financial advance for them.

Marriage itself is not necessarily an institution of economic equality. A homemaker who looks after the family so that her husband can hold a paid job may be completely dependent on him financially. If he is generous, she is fortunate, but if he is stingy, her life can be miserable. Even if the husband is generous, his single salary may not be sufficient to keep the family out of poverty if the wife must stay home to look after young children.

The majority of low-income families in Canada have paid work. The problem is that it is often minimum wage work, and the minimum wage tends to be lower than the poverty line established for a person with a child. For example in 2006, a woman working 40 hours per week, 50 weeks a year, for the minimum wage of $7.75 in Ontario earned $15,500. The estimated poverty line for a woman with a child for 2004 was $17,364 in a rural area and $25,127 in a metropolitan area (National Council of Welfare 2004). Then there are thousands of husbands who are unemployed. The only way for these low-income families to keep out of poverty is for the wife to get a paid job (Bergmann 1987). Many working mothers would prefer to remain at home with their small children, but they cannot afford to do so—either for financial reasons or for fear of jeopardizing their job security and advancement (Sprankle 1986).

If a wife's earnings are deducted from the incomes of Canadian families and the remaining income is compared with the poverty lines, the result is an astounding 50 to 60 percent rise in poor families (National Council of Welfare 2004). Increasingly, family income is becoming a product of the earnings of both spouses, and it is only when their combined efforts to earn enough income fail that family poverty becomes inevitable.

The dissolution of marriage

There is a crucial interaction between dissolution of marriage and its impact on female poverty. Canadian laws proclaim equality in the case of dissolution of marriage—where all the family assets are divided equally. But that is

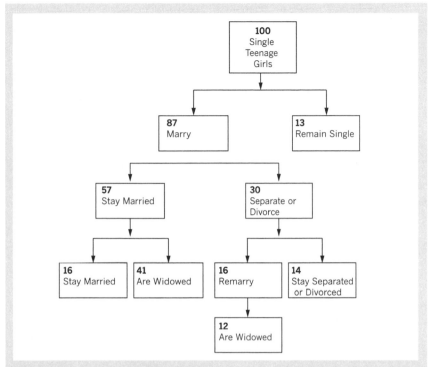

4-1 Life Patterns of Canadian Women

Source: National Council of Welfare. 1990. *Women and Poverty Revisited*. Ottawa: National Council of Welfare, 26.

only part of the picture. Demographers use the concept of life expectancy to study patterns of marriage over the lifetime of a cohort of women assumed to be born at the same time. An example, based on Statistics Canada data, is presented in Figure 4-1. According to this construct, if 100 Canadian women are followed over their lifetime, 87 of them will get married and 13 will remain single. Out of the 87 married women, 57 will remain married and 30 will get separated or divorced. Out of the 57 women who remain married, 41 will outlive their husband. This means that only 16 percent of Canadian women can expect to live in two-spouse families throughout their life, whereas 84 percent of them can expect at some point in their life to have to meet their economic needs without the aid of a spouse's income and/or pension. Most of the young girls who send their Barbie doll to the marriage altar with her very loving boyfriend Ken are likely to eventually face life without marriage due to divorce or the death of their spouse. To crown these broken dreams, a high proportion of the 67 out of 100 women whose marriage will have ended due to separation, divorce, or death of the husband will find themselves in the clutches of poverty.

Factors before marriage seem to be as important as factors after marriage for explaining poverty among single female parents. Age at marriage seems to be an important predictor of poverty among single parents. Many women who ultimately divorce tend to marry very young, and women who married young were more likely to have low levels of education and large families (Waite and Moore 1978). As a result of low education, many divorced women find it difficult to get a well-paying job (Hewlett 1986). This is true because age at marriage is correlated with the probability of divorce (Rotz 2004) and education with income.

A number of studies suggest that low-income couples are more likely to separate or divorce and that many divorced women remain poor because they were poor before the break-up of their marriage (Hannan, Tuma, and Groeneveld 1977).

Post-marital factors such as default by ex-husbands on court-ordered payments, presence of young children, and lower welfare benefits, are the major hindrances in the way of single parents which keep them trapped in poverty (Beaujot and Liu 2004). The Law Reform Commission reported in 1976 that half of court-ordered support payments were never made. Even today, in any given month, just over two-thirds of cases are in full compliance with their regular child or spousal support payments (Statistics Canada 17 September 2010). In the absence of adequately subsidized child care services, it is difficult for single mothers to look for a paid job. Welfare becomes an unavoidable alternative in the absence of a paid job. Of course, welfare payments invariably fall short of poverty lines (National Council of Welfare 2005).

We have already seen that due to higher life expectancy and lower age at marriage among women, a large proportion of them experience widowhood. Many women are ill-prepared to deal with widowhood. In a house-to-house survey in suburban Toronto, 41 percent of the women had no idea of the type of pension they could expect to get at age 65 (National Council of Welfare 1979). The awareness of pension plans among many women is still very low (Morissette and Zhang 2004). In most cases, a woman receives only 50 percent of her husband's pension entitlement after his death, and her years of unpaid service to the household are rewarded with poverty in the golden years.

Women and the labour market

Though it is difficult to support with hard data, it will not be wrong to assume that most women today work for 5 to 10 years before having a child and work for 30-odd years in total until retirement. The crucial factor that determines what job a woman will hold is her level of education.

Prolonged gender discrimination leaves women concentrated in low-skilled and low-paid occupations (Armstrong and Armstrong 1987). Though increasingly higher education and affirmative action legislation are of some help to women, the beneficiaries still seem to be very few. As discussed in Chapter 2, on ethnic poverty, recent immigrant women face barriers to decent employment in spite of their high education. The majority of women in Canada who have jobs in the labour market work in such traditionally female-dominated occupations as clerical services, sales, health services, and teaching. Women are more likely than men to work for the small, non-unionized, and precarious business sector of the economy that does not provide job security or employment benefits (Jackson 2004). This occupational segregation, which we might term *occupational ghettoization*, is conducive to conditions of poverty.

Today's "occupational ghettoization" of women in fact is rooted in the traditional power structure of society. Men as a group traditionally worked outside the home and controlled the power resources of the wider society, and women worked inside the home and consequently wielded little power in the larger society. Women's domestic work, being unpaid, is considered of minimal value by a society that equates worth with money (Gee and Kimball 1987). Even when women work outside the home, their work is viewed secondary to the primary role of homemaker, and, thus, women have a devalued role in our society (Gee and Kimball 1987). Women in 2008 earned only 65 percent of men's earnings (Statistics Canada 24 February 2012), which implies that lacking economic power, women remain at a high risk of poverty.

Pay equity and affirmative action

Pay equity legislation is meant to eliminate the inequality caused by systemic discrimination in the workplace. On 25 June 1987, the Canadian Human Rights Commission issued details on pay equity. There are three levels of pay equity (Kelly 1988):

- Equal pay for equal work: requires that male and female employees be paid the same wage for doing identical work. For example, a waiter and a waitress are required to be paid the same wage. This legislation exists in every province in Canada.
- Equal pay for similar or substantially similar work: implies that male and female employees should be paid equal wages if they have different job titles but perform substantially the same work. For example, a male janitor and a female cleaner should be paid the same wage. This legislation also exists in every Canadian province.

- Equal pay for work of equal value: this concept does not compare "work" but, rather, the "value" of the work. Dissimilar jobs are compared by determining the "value" of work using evaluation techniques. Difficulty in equating jobs is insurmountable when there are no male maids and seamstresses.

Despite pay equity legislations, we are still far away from affirmative action legislation that benefits ethnic minorities and recent immigrant women. Therefore, ethnic and recent immigrant women continue to be in a disadvantageous position in the Canadian labour force because of their double minority status. A Royal Commission background report on equality in employment known as the Abella Report concluded that well-trained and experienced, skilled workers and professionals of minority background are unfairly penalized for lack of Canadian experience and by artificially high requirements for certification or credentials (Buckland 1985). This affects professional visible minority women even more adversely. When every other avenue fails, many skilled and professional women of visible minority background settle either for low-paid, substandard jobs or for looking after the household.

Millions of part-time workers need the protection of affirmative action (Coates 1988). In Canada, part-time workers are predominantly women, and part-time work is heavily concentrated in the low-paid service sector of the economy, which does not carry private pension plans (Gee and Kimball 1987), thus making women more vulnerable to poverty in their old age as well. There are millions of women in working poor families who need the protection of affirmative action, yet employment equity legislation does not exist in most provinces. The pioneer effort in Ontario was reversed by the Conservative government in 1995.

The domestic double standard

Women are caught in a vicious circle. Domestic work remains the exclusive jurisdiction even of those women whose husbands can get well-paid jobs (Sprankle 1986). Their work outside the home is considered secondary. Men increase their contribution to housework and child care by an average of only one hour when their wives work outside the home (Ram October 1987). Though child care programs are improving in Canada, they are still fledgling outside of Quebec. It is the woman who has to alter her work schedule when child care arrangements fail or children fall sick (Armstrong and Armstrong 1978). A survey found that in the 41 percent of the cases where a spouse did not help in child care decision making, the woman made career sacrifices in an effort to achieve a balance between her obligation to child care and to her career (Salsberg Ezryn 1989). Under such societal circumstances, women will continue to be segregated in dead-end jobs, and women's improved education will not bring a desired return in the labour market.

The daycare dilemma

A large proportion of women in poverty are single parents. If the rate of marital dissolution continues to increase, even at a slower pace, the demand for daycare by lone-parent families is going to be much larger. According to Ram (October 1987), 60 percent of the 5.3 million children in Canada need daycare and half a million of these children live in lone-parent families.

A 1981 survey by Statistics Canada found that 31 percent of all children were cared for by relatives and 41 percent by non-relatives, including friends and neighbours (Ram August 1986). This means that a large proportion of children were still out of formal daycare. It was difficult to estimate precisely how many children in Canada are subsidized by various federal, provincial, and municipal agencies. The situation for daycare availability remains grim. A report by Statistics Canada (2006b) concluded that 53 percent of Canadian children under the age of five in 2002 were in daycare. With the exception of Quebec, there is a dearth of subsidized daycare all over the country. This reinforces the importance of building an effective child care system in Canada to help working mothers.

Most of government funding for child care is given in the form of subsidies to low-income families, and is consequently perceived as a welfare service. Daycare assistance to single mothers is an alternative that may reverse the "feminization of poverty." Only when single mothers are able to work are they likely to escape poverty. Women's role in keeping families out of poverty deserves a special mention. The National Council of Welfare (2004) reported that in 2001 without women's earnings, two-parent families with children under the age of 18 would have had a poverty rate of 20.2 percent, compared with the actual rate of 5.2 percent. In absolute terms, this means that there would have been 508,000 such poor families instead of 131,000.

The paradox of the double strike

Though all women in Canada are at a higher risk of poverty than men, certain women however, are doubly disadvantaged because they are also rural women, Aboriginal women, immigrant women, visible minority women, disabled women, or adolescent women. Torjman, in her 1987 report on what she terms *the reality gap*, addresses the disadvantageous position of these women in terms of needs and availability of programs and services. There is no recent study available that replicates Torjman's (1987) work, but it can be assumed that the recent picture may not be very different from the following discussion that is derived from this study.

Rural women

The isolation of and lack of services for rural women has been documented in the areas of shelter, child care, mental health, and physical health. There has been a serious shortage of shelters for battered women in Canada (MacLeod 1987). A study conducted in rural Ontario pointed out that mental health needs for a community of 56,000 were served by only one psychiatrist and one agency (Hundermark 1985). Rural women usually suffered enormous stress because they were overworked, were considerably underpaid, and performed the major responsibility of child rearing (Torjman 1987). The availability of treatment and prevention services for accidents is minimal in rural areas compared with the high risk of accidents due to dangerous machinery, chemicals, gases, and large animals (Torjman 1987). In rural areas where families are under great stress, women become victims of physical abuse and poverty more often than do those living in metropolitan areas. Social programs and services often have high levels of urban bias and do little to alleviate the misery of many poor rural women.

Aboriginal women

We have discussed conditions of poverty among the Aboriginal population of Canada in Chapter 2, on ethnic poverty. In addition to being vulnerable to poverty because of their minority status, Aboriginal women are vulnerable to poverty because many of them are single parents. The existing programs and services for Aboriginal women do not take into account their linguistic and cultural background (Torjman 1987). For example, most of the time, they are not designed to consider the role of elders in raising children.

Immigrant women

A major study in Toronto on the needs of immigrants showed that many immigrant women were unaware of many services in Canada (Sharma 1980). For example, many immigrant women qualified for child care subsidies, yet never applied because they did not know about subsidy programs (Mock 1986). Many child care programs also tend to be "unicultural" and do not provide learning environments that reflect diverse cultural backgrounds. Many immigrant women are forced to consider informal care over formal care because they are employed in the manufacturing and service sectors, which require these women to be at work early in the morning, or in the evening, or on weekends (Torjman 1987).

Immigrant women's marked economic disadvantage is reflected by higher unemployment rates, concentration in low-skilled, low-paid, and vulnerable sectors of the labour market (Buckland 1985). Low status in the labour market is a barrier to economic mobility as immigrant women are unable to upgrade their skills because of low salaries, work-related demands, and child care responsibilities.

A study on Canadian Portuguese women revealed that there were no mental health services available to many battered women (Torjman 1987, 35). Poor, battered, "doubly disadvantaged" in the labour market, and alien to the culture, many immigrant women still perform jobs that Canadian-born women do not want to take.

Visible minority women

Visible minority women face double discrimination because of their sex and their colour or race. They have difficulty finding employment and experience difficulties related to promotions, income security, and adequate housing (Torjman 1987). Discrimination limits their choice in the labour market and their opportunities for advancement (Buckland 1985).

Visible minority single-parent women face a serious housing problem. Finding suitable accommodation becomes insurmountable because of three major barriers: low incomes, anti-family attitudes, and discrimination based on race and colour (Torjman 1987). There are few services available which effectively respond to this "double strike" against these women.

Disabled women

According to Torjman (1987), disabled women face multiple problems because they do not seem to fit the traditional female role of a wage earner. No culturally valued roles are considered valuable for them, and hence, they are discriminated against in the workplace. The result of the "double strike" against them is high unemployment and low income.

Adolescent women

Teenage pregnancies are a result of denial or unavailability of family planning and contraceptive services to adolescent women. As was discussed above, once an adolescent woman becomes a mother, it usually means dropping out of school and the beginning a life of poverty. Because they are considered "minors" under the law, they are denied social assistance, family planning services, public housing, or child care services on the grounds that they themselves require protection (Torjman 1987). These services are denied to adolescent women because of the public belief that the extension of services will cause them to behave in an undesirable way; that is, they will run away from home or have an epidemic of babies (Torjman 1987). Adolescent women usually run away to escape from violent or incestuous family relations. And then they are denied alternatives because they are treated as though they were the perpetrators, rather than the victims, of family problems (Torjman 1987). If an appropriate network of social services to adolescent women were established to help them to complete their education, most of these women would avoid poverty in their adulthood. These services could act as important measures of prevention of poverty among women.

The poverty of millions of women is shared by their children. The impact of poverty is even more severe on children as they pay a price for their parents' poverty in the form of mental, physical, social, and economic development. In the next chapter, we turn to the hundreds of thousands of Canadian children in poverty.

Conceptual Explanation

The concept that seems to be helpful in explaining poverty among women is social exclusion. Traditionally, men worked outside and women worked inside the home. In most societies, work inside the home is not considered prestigious because no compensation is attached to domestic work, which also includes care of children. It was during World War II, when men were away fighting, that women were required to work in factories to support the family and to sustain the war effort. This was the beginning of workforce participation by women in Western societies. Because women's traditional domestic work was undervalued by the society, when they started to work outside of the home their work continued to be undervalued. Even today, in Canada women are paid only 65 percent of men's wage (Statistics Canada 24 February 2012), and they do more unpaid work, which includes housework, child care, meal preparation, and eldercare (Veerle 2011). In order to juggle their domestic responsibilities, many women choose part-time, seasonal, contract, or temporary jobs, which are low paid (Canadian Women's Foundation 2011). Clustering women in low-paid jobs is the major source of exclusion. Aboriginal, immigrant, visible minority, elderly, and disabled women are not only clustered in low-paid jobs, they also suffer exclusion due to discrimination.

According to Statistics Canada (2006b), 28 percent of Aboriginal women lived on-reserve. Although the proportion of Aboriginal women working in sales and services was close to that of non-Aboriginal women, a much higher percentage of Aboriginal women compared with non-Aboriginal women were unemployed (Statistics Canada 2006b). Aboriginal women suffer from labour force exclusion as result of geographical isolation and a high unemployment rate. Immigrant women are likely to have high unemployment rates and are more likely to be concentrated in traditional female jobs. Visible minority women also share these characteristics of immigrant women and many also experience discrimination (Statistics Canada 2006b). Many elderly women live alone and depend on government transfer payments. Women suffer exclusion because they are relegated to unpaid or low-paid jobs and many are discriminated against based on their ethnicity, gender, age, and disability.

Chapter 5

Children in Poverty

Introduction

An all-party resolution committed the Government of Canada (24 November 1989) to seek to eliminate child poverty by the year 2000. Yet, in 2009, among 2.3 million poor Canadians, 28 percent were children (Statistics Canada June 2011a). Children are the future workforce of the country. Child poverty affects future workforce outcomes adversely because of its negative influence on children's education and health. In a highly competitive global economy, this should be a national worry. Poverty robs a child of an equal chance to rise as far as his or her abilities allow—a fundamental right vehemently professed by democratic societies. Poverty denies a child this right.

The recessions of the 1980s and the 1990s had a strong impact on child poverty in Canada. The percentage of children living in poverty peaked at 18.4 percent in 1996 and then steadily declined to 9.5 percent in 2009 (Table 5-1). Canada has not been as successful in reducing poverty among its children as it has been among its elderly. Over the period of 1990–2009, the rate of poverty among Canadian elderly has been reduced by 108 percent, from 10.8 to 5.2 percent, but child poverty has declined by only 47 percent, from 14.0 to 9.5 percent (Statistics Canada June 2011a). With some cyclic variations during economic recessions and recoveries, the poverty rate of children in Canada has been pretty tenacious for more than 30 years (Campaign2000 2005). This chapter attempts to unravel this perplexing paradox of Canadian social policy.

The Profile of Child Poverty in Canada

Table 5-1 highlights child poverty rates for years marked by economic fluctuation in Canada. The years 1983, 1993, and 1996 were marked by

Table 5-1 Trends in Child Poverty in Canada, Selected Years

Year	Number of Poor Children	Percent of Poor Children
1983	1,020,000	13.9
1989	765,000	11.5
1993	1,180,000	17.0
1996	1,293,000	18.4
2002	851,000	12.4
2006	768,000	11.4
2007	643,000	9.6
2008	610,000	9.1
2009	639,000	9.5

Source: Statistics Canada. June 2011a. "CANSIM Table 202-0802." *Persons in Low Income after Tax.* Statistics Canada Catalogue no. 75-202-X. Ottawa: Statistics Canada.

economic recession, and 1989 and 2002 saw economic recovery. Numbers of poor children and their poverty rates are affected by economic fluctuations because poor children are more likely to be living in families where parents are more likely to be vulnerable to the vagaries of the economy. Recently, the declining trend in the child poverty rate seems to have reversed in 2009 due to the economic slowdown of 2008 (Table 5-1).

Child poverty by family type

It is the parents' lack of access to a decent job that keeps their children in poverty. The access to jobs varies with the economic cycle. In two-parent families, 1 in every 9 children was in poverty during the recession years of 1983 and 1993 (Table 5-2). Because economic recovery helps alleviate child poverty by improving the job prospects of parents, in 1989 and 2002, 1 out of every 14 children was poor (Table 5-2). The picture was very different in female lone-parent families. During the recession years of 1983 and 1996, 1 in every 2 children in female lone-parent families lived in poverty, and during the recovery years of 1989 and 2002, 1 in almost out of every 2.5 children were poor. In other words, during the recovery years, more female parents in two-parent families are able to supplement their family income. However, most of the mothers in single-parent families remain out of the labour force irrespective of recession or economic expansion.

In the literature on poverty, when single parents are discussed, hardly any mention is made of their children, who suffer equally as much as, if not more than, their parents. Children living in families headed by female lone

Table 5-2   Poor Children by Family Type, Selected Years

	Two-Parent Families		Female Lone Parents		All Other Families	
	Number	Percent	Number	Percent	Number	Percent
1983	613,000	10.7	340,000	56.1	67,000	28.9
1989	400,000	7.0	326,000	47.8	40,000	16.1
1993	603,000	10.7	490,000	49.6	63,000	25.1
1996	661,000	11.6	555,000	56.0	60,000	23.1
2002	408,000	7.4	397,000	43.0	37,000	11.2
2006	415,000	7.7	302,000	31.7	38,000	11.2
2009	396,000	7.3	196,000	21.5	36,000	11.2

Source: Statistics Canada. June 2011a.. "CANSIM Table 202-0802." *Persons in Low Income after Tax.* Statistics Canada Catalogue no. 75-202-X. Ottawa: Statistics Canada. Last modified 15 June 2011. Available online.

parents are at the highest risk of poverty. Though there is a declining trend in family poverty overall, the numbers differ depending on family situation. In 2009, more than 1 in 5 children living in female lone-parent families were poor, compared with 1 in 13 in two-parent families (Table 5-2).

Divorce has been reported to have an adverse effect on children's adjustment. Ram and Hou (2003) found that children in lone-parent families and step-parent families are at a disadvantage in cognitive and emotional development compared with children in two-parent families. They also reported that parents who suffered an income loss due to divorce or separation were not able to provide children with the school supplies, computers, and high-quality daycare that might help children improve and maintain academic ability. Because education is positively related to income, poverty among children in lone-parent families may become an important factor in perpetuating poverty from one generation to another. It may not be divorce or separation but the ensuing poverty which affects children adversely.

Consequences of Child Poverty

Poverty affects children's health and their performance in school. Even as far back as 1975, a report by the National Council of Welfare concluded that to be born poor is to face a greater likelihood of ill health, little education, being judged a delinquent in adolescence—in other words, having the deck stacked against you at birth to find life an uphill struggle thereafter. A dry numerical analysis of the type so often carried out by the community of social scientists blurs the picture of more than six hundred thousand poor children who are growing up in Canada without as much food, toys, clothes, and outings as their non-poor counterparts. Numbers swallow up the individual realities that together make up poverty. The following is a glimpse of such a reality described by Pierre from northern New Brunswick:

> I'm 13 years old. I'm the eldest of seven children. What makes me suffer most is not having a house, having to live in a shack where it's always cold and too small for all the family. There are nine of us. The seven children all sleep together in two 36" wide beds—pushed together in winter for more heat since we don't have enough blankets. We have an old broken-down stove. In the winter we push the beds near the stove, but it's dangerous.
>
> Autumn isn't very much fun either. It's cold also, and the rats come in—you have to watch so they won't bite the smaller children. This week they chewed off part of the pump so we have no water and the neighbours tell us their well is low, so we do without water. We're not always clean when we go to school. (National Council of Welfare 1975, 8–9)

Not all of the poor children in Canada need to cope with rats, and for many the reality of poverty is perhaps less dramatic. But the effects of poverty are still destructive. Here is what a 14-year-old boy from Quebec has to say:

> I love sports but I can't participate in anything because we have no money for equipment. We never do anything because of lack of money. I feel as if it will always be this way. (National Council of Welfare 1975, 8–9)

Duncan and Brooks-Gunn (in JRank 2008) have summarized extensive research findings that substantiate a significant association between poverty and children's health, cognitive development, behaviour problems, emotional well-being, and problems with school achievement. According to JRank (2008), children from poor families are 1.7 times more likely to be born with low birth weight, two times more likely to repeat a grade in school, two times more likely to drop out of school, and more than three times more likely to have an out-of-wedlock birth than children from non-poor families. The main areas of concern for children in poverty are health, education, nutrition, psychological well-being, housing, and recreation.

Health and children in poverty

The effects of poverty often begin even before the birth of a poor child. Poverty is the greatest adversary of a child's health. Ill health in childhood affects the adulthood health and economic prospects of a person. Physical and mental development of the foetus can be affected by the mother's poor diet during pregnancy, and an adequate diet is often beyond the financial reach of a poor mother. There is no doubt that poor children start paying the price of their poverty in stunted growth even before they are born. A British national study of 16,000 children found that poor children were more likely to be born underweight and premature (Wedge and Prosser 1973). Shah, Kahan, and Krauser (1987) reviewed the literature and reported the following risks associated with poverty among Canadian children.

Infant mortality

If Canadian families are divided into five quintiles based on income, infant mortality (deaths during first year of children's life) is one and a half times higher for children born in families in the lowest quintile than for the children born in families in the highest quintile.

First Nations children are at even more of a disadvantage when it comes to survival during their first year of life. In 1983, the infant mortality rate for First Nations children was twice the national average. For Inuit children it was four times the national average. The post-neonatal mortality rate (the infant death rate during the first month after birth) was almost four times higher for First Nations and Inuit infants than the national average. Between 1983 and 2001, the infant mortality rate among the Aboriginal population overall declined from 18 to 7. However, despite this impressive decline, the levels of morbidity and mortality among First Nations children and youth on-reserve remain high throughout their first 18 years of life (National Council of Welfare 2007).

Childhood mortality

According to Shah, Kahan, and Krauser (1987), in 1981 the mortality rate for boys 1 to 14 years old from families in the lowest one-fifth income group was almost two times higher than that in the highest one-fifth income group. It was two and a half times higher for girls. Aboriginal children in this age group had much higher mortality rate than non-Aboriginal children. In 1982, the mortality rate for First Nations children under the age of four years was almost three times the rate for non-Aboriginal children, and the accidental death rate for children aged 5 to 14 was three times the national average (Shah, Kahan, and Krauser 1987).

In 1999, the infant mortality rate for First Nations populations was one and a half times higher than that of other infants in Canada (Health Canada 2002b). In addition, the rate of deaths from injuries was three to four times higher for Aboriginal children than for other children in Canada

(Health Canada 2002b). Persistent high levels of sudden infant death syndrome have also been documented among Aboriginal children (Canadian Institute of Child Health 2000).

Accidents and self-injury

Accidents, suicide, and homicide take more lives of poor children than of non-poor children. Poor children are almost five times more likely to die from pedestrian–automobile collisions and drowning than children from higher-income families (Shah, Kahan, and Krauser 1987). Suicide and homicide rates are three to four times higher for poor children than for non-poor children (Dougherty 1986). Higher suicide rates among the poor are explained by the hopelessness and dead-end mentality created by the conditions of poverty. Suicide rates are five to six times higher for First Nations youth than for non-Aboriginal youth in Canada (National Council of Welfare 2007).

Cancer

The risk of death from cancer among Canadian children under the age of 14 was more than twice as high in the lowest income quintile as in the highest income quintile (Shah, Kahan, and Krauser 1987). Similarly, the two-year survival rate for children with lymphoblastic leukemia was 28 percent for those on the lowest rungs of the socio-economic ladder and 51 percent for those in a high income group (McWhirter, Smith, and McWhirter 1983). Poor children have a lower rate of survival from this disease because they tend to get diagnosed at the advanced stages of the disease and have inadequate access to health care and have poor nutrition (Shah, Kahan, and Krauser 1987).

Infectious diseases

Poor children were also found to be at a much higher risk for infectious diseases because resistance to infections is affected by the combined impact of health conditions and nutrition. Dougherty (1986) found that pneumonia in children aged 1 to 14 years was two times more prevalent among boys and six times higher among girls from low-income families as compared with boys and girls from high-income families.

The incidence of infectious diseases was much higher among First Nations children. A survey found that the number of hospital admissions among First Nations children was seven times higher than the national average (DIAND 1980). The incidence of pneumonia was found to be more than eight times higher among First Nations children of two years of age compared with non-Aboriginal children of the same age (Ever and Rand 1983). The incidence of meningitis for First Nations and Inuit children in the Northwest

Territories was reported to be approximately 200 times higher than in the general population in the first eight years of life (Shah, Kahan, and Krauser 1987). The incidence of gastroenteritis, tuberculosis, diphtheria, and rheumatic fever was also found to be higher among First Nations children than among non-Aboriginal children (Shah, Kahan, and Krauser 1987).

Mental health

Poverty generates stress on children and parents and disrupts proper functioning of a family. High stress is related to domestic violence and child abuse. A study conducted in Ontario (Offord, Boyle, and Jones 1987) found that parents' being on social assistance can be used as a marker for identifying children with psychiatric disorders and poor school performance. The prevalence of psychiatric disorders among boys aged 6 to 11 whose families were on welfare was 40 percent, compared with 14 percent for boys whose families were not on welfare. As discussed in Chapter 1, the stigma of welfare interferes with the development of self-esteem, adversely affects school performance, and may initiate intergenerational poverty.

Access to medical care

There is no doubt that medical care is not as accessible to the poor as it is to the non-poor in most societies of the world. But in Canada, universal medical care is supposed to provide equal access to medical care among various income groups. Many of the studies quoted earlier show that poor children continue to have a higher incidence of illness. Free access to health care alone is not sufficient for transforming the health of the poor children because though most drugs are free for the poor in Canada, the preventive and early pain relieving drugs, such as children's Aspirin, are not free. Some categories of prescription drugs also are not free for many poor children. Even before reaching a doctor, a poor person who does not own a car would need a taxi, and a poor mother with a sick child may even need a baby-sitter for the children left at home. None of these come free. The resulting inaccessibility to health care is another reason for poor health outcomes among children in poverty.

Nutrition and growth of poor children

The Special Senate Committee on Poverty made it quite clear in its 1971 report that dietary inadequacies and under-nutrition are linked to anaemia, low-resistance to infectious diseases, mental retardation, and mental impairment. This report points out that under-nourishment directly reduces a child's ability to acquire an education to escape poverty because the distractions caused by nagging pangs of hunger interfere with their concentration required to learn.

Poor children may not suffer from starvation, but they surely suffer from an imbalanced diet. The Nutrition Canada Survey revealed that the mean intake of all nutrients, especially vitamins C and A, foliate, and calcium is directly related to family income (Mayer 1978). Children of low-income families were more likely to have an iron deficiency (Singer 1982). The lack of vitamin D, which is found in dairy products, can cause rickets, a condition that makes bones brittle. Lack of iron—found in red meat, greens, and nuts—leads to impaired hemoglobin, which is the cause of premature fatigue as blood fails to use oxygen properly.

Educational attainment and child poverty

Many studies have found an inverse relationship between education and poverty. A McMaster University study of 3,000 children found that children from welfare families were four times more likely to fail a grade than children from middle-class families (Stefaniuk 1989). This study also reported that 28 percent of girls between 6 and 11 years of age from welfare families performed poorly in school, compared with only 6 percent of those from non-welfare families.

Prior to 1993, Ontario children were streamed into basic, general, and advanced level courses in grade nine. A Toronto Board of Education survey conducted in 1983 indicated that 88 percent of children from middle-class families, compared with only 46 percent of children from the low-income families, were in the advanced stream, which leads to university education (Stefaniuk 1989). Again, the pattern is far more pronounced among Aboriginal children. The poor educational attainment and difficulties in education of Aboriginal children have been discussed in Chapter 2, on ethnic poverty under the subheading of "Families."

Higher education is the only source of future well-being for a large majority of Canadians (Stefaniuk 1989). Why do poor children tend to aspire so low and drop out first? Why do they end up achieving far less than their mental ability would allow them to? A report of the National Council of Welfare provided the answers to these nagging questions as far back as 1975. According to this report, poor children are more likely to come to school underfed, or even hungry. A hungry child is less likely to concentrate and learn. The report quotes a British study that reveals that poor children missed school more due to illness—1 in 50 poor children, compared with 1 in 250 non-poor children missed school for more than three months in a year due to illness.

Poor children not only have a much higher likelihood of being born underweight and premature, they are also likely to be born into families which invariably face a short supply of food, crowded housing, and inadequate warm clothing. All these conditions affect educational attainment adversely. Here is another quote from a Canadian teenage girl:

> During the winter I lined my shoes since I had no boots. But the snow kept getting in, so I had flu all winter. (National Council of Welfare 1975, 21)

The National Council of Welfare (1975) report contends that the implications of these living conditions are overwhelming. For example, in a crowded household, when one child gets the flu, he or she is more likely to transmit it to others. Moreover, a mother unable to buy boots is left with no option but to keep a child at home when snow falls. And a working poor parent can't stay home without losing a day's wages. Therefore, many times a poor child has to stay home to look after a younger sick sibling. This impacts the poor child's education and learning.

School is the place where the stigma of poverty becomes manifested among children (Waxman 1977). But when the stigma of welfare hits poor children, the only escape they think of is to drop out and to find a job. Inner city schools, where poor children are likely to go in their primary grades, are more likely to have a homogenous population. However, the secondary school situation is unlikely to provide poor children with the same insulation of being surrounded by other poor children. The following description reveals vividly that it is in school where the stigma of being poor becomes a harsh reality for a poor child:

> He learns that school is where the class project on what-I-did-on-my-summer-vacation that tells him how different he is. School is where the other kids wear the latest fashions and the poor kid learns how conspicuous she is in her second-hand clothes. . . . school is where he fears to make new friends because he is ashamed for them to see his home, and school is where she is ashamed to go to the class dance because she has nothing appropriate to wear. . . . school is where the special class outings cost . . . a dollar that the poor kid hasn't got. . . . school is where the kids swap tales of what they got for . . . birthdays and the poor kid learns that he isn't like everyone else. . . .
> School is where the poor kid . . . finds that he's been left out. (National Council of Welfare 1975, 22)

Another experience of poor children is that they find themselves more often in the slow-learner classes—the classes that don't take them very far in a highly competitive society (National Council of Welfare 1975).

The home life of poor children

Housing for poor children ranges from an unheated, rundown cabin without running water in a Northern Canadian community to an apartment in a high-rise public housing building in a metropolis. A large proportion of Canada's poor live in urban areas, where low-rent housing is extremely difficult to find. In cities, a small fraction of the poor are able to obtain accommodation in public housing, and a large section of the poor end up living in over-crowded, decaying, rundown buildings (Black 1989a). Poverty for children has serious implications because it puts a strain on them during their formative years. The strain of poverty on parents is likely to affect the home atmosphere. The likelihood of personal dysfunction, such as mental illness and alcoholism, is evenly distributed among social classes, but the extent to which the dysfunction is manifested depends upon the stresses experienced by a person (National Council of Welfare 1975). Poverty may not generate dysfunction in all of the poor because a human's resilience to cope with economic crisis is quite high. But many of the poor who would have been able to cope with the lesser tensions of a non-poor lifestyle are likely to succumb to the high stresses of poverty.

A large number of children who live in foster homes also come from poor homes. A British study (Wedge and Prosser 1973) showed that poor children are 10 times more likely to be placed in alternative care than are non-poor children. Disrupted family life makes family cohesion impossible. Another segment of poor children is the homeless children. If a child does leave home before the age of 15, in almost every case it is because of sexual or violent abuse, and because an abused child feels safer on the street than at home (*Homeless People—Rebecca's Story* 2008).

This is Rebecca's experience, in her own words:

Two things happened when I turned 12, my Father who used to beat the hell out of us left home and the other thing that happened is I started using drugs. . . . One of my friends said "Here try this it will make you feel better," and it did.

When I turned 13, my Mum found a new partner who lived at home with us. He raped me regularly and abused my younger sisters as well. I was only 13.

He also used to beat Mum up and it was hell on earth. For about a year I suffered through it but when I was fourteen I couldn't take it anymore, so I said to Mum "You have to get rid of this guy, either he goes or I go." Mum chose him and I landed on the streets. (*Homeless People—Rebecca's Story* 2008)

Delinquency and childhood poverty

A survey of 3,000 Canadians found that poverty has a major impact on the psychological development of children (Black 1989b). According to this study, 46 percent of boys aged 6 to 11 whose parents were on welfare suffered from a psychological disorder, compared with 14 percent of the boys whose parents were not on welfare. Among girls aged 12 to 16 whose parents were on welfare, 40 percent suffered from such disorders, compared with 17 percent of girls whose parents were not on welfare. This study also found higher rates of psychiatric disorders in children whose parents were on welfare (31 percent) than in children whose parents were not on welfare (14 percent). The prevalence of childhood emotional and behavioural problems is significantly associated with poverty (Lipman, Offord, and Dooley 1996).

Recreation and culture

The lack of recreation facilities for children in poverty is another reality that may result in delinquent activities among poor children. According to a survey conducted by the Saskatchewan Department of Social Services (1974), about 80 percent of parents on welfare with school age children reported inaccessibility of safe and adequate play space. The lack of accessibility to recreational activities is directly associated with the cost of activities. The $30 to $35 for a half-hour music lesson, $200 per term for ballet classes, or $400 for a 20-week program of drama classes in cities such as Toronto are out of the reach of a poor child. These experiences, common for many middle-class children, are only a dream for children of poor families (Dunphy 1989).

In light of these circumstances, it should not be surprising if poor children were resentful, street smart, and hardened, and without adequate recreational facilities were more frequently delinquent than non-poor children (National Council of Welfare 1975).

Child Poverty and Public Policy

Before we discuss what should be done, let us review the snapshot of child poverty in Canada from the 2005 report card of Campaign2000, an organization that prepares the annual update on child poverty in Canada. According to this report card:

* almost 1 in every 6 children in Canada are poor;
* the child poverty rate has remained unchanged since 2000, despite economic growth;

- low-income couples with children have incomes on average $9,900 below the poverty line; poor lone mothers would need on average of $9,600 to reach the poverty line;
- in 2004, 41 percent of food bank users were children; and
- child poverty rates for Aboriginal, immigrant, and visible minority groups and for children with disabilities are more than double the average for all children.

These five points indicate that child poverty remains a serious issue in Canada and that social exclusion of Aboriginal, recent immigrant, and visible minority groups, and of children with disabilities, has worsened. What can be done to reduce child poverty in a developed country like Canada? Albanese (2010) explores causes of child poverty and provides detailed solutions and recommendations for change. Campaign2000 (2005) also alludes to several areas of improvement in the economic and social sphere. Brief summaries of the sections of this study relating to minimum wage, social inequality, social spending, and the special case of vulnerable children are presented below.

The labour market: A pathway out of poverty for families

In 1990, the Economic Council of Canada published a landmark study entitled *Good Jobs, Bad Jobs*. This study asserted that in the 1980s most employment growth took place in the service sector and that due to the very nature of this sector, these jobs were either high-paid, high-tech jobs or low-paid, low-tech, predominantly part-time jobs. Since the restructuring and downsizing of 1990s, many good jobs have been replaced by non-standard, part-time, contract, and seasonal employment (Campaign2000 2005). The latest information shows that one-third of all poor children in Canada live in families with at least one parent working full-time, full year (Canadian Council of Social Development quoted in Campaign2000 2005). This indicates either that minimum wage policies need to be amended or that working poor parents must be provided with income supplements to lift one-third of poor children over the poverty threshold.

Minimum wage and child poverty

In Canada, minimum wage legislation was introduced in the early 20th century in British Columbia and Manitoba to protect the most vulnerable workers, namely, women and children. It was later extended to men, and eventually minimum wage legislation became prevalent in all Canadian provinces as employment standards became more widespread. There are two divergent views on the minimum wage. One argument is that it is an important tool to alleviate poverty and enhance social welfare; based on this argument, it is urged that the minimum wage be set at a rate where the basic needs of workers may be adequately met (Battle 2003; Greenberg and Green 1999; Black and Shaw 1998). The other argument is that the minimum wage inhibits employment creation and increases poverty because too high a minimum wage can artificially increase the cost of labour and is thus detrimental to the very people it is meant to help (Law and Mihlar 1998). According to this argument, the increase in the minimum wage would reduce the demand for workers because employers will find them more costly, and it may also increase the supply of workers because some workers who previously did not find minimum wage jobs attractive would be encouraged to consider them, resulting in a reduction in employment and an increase in the unemployment rate (Sarlo 2000; Law and Mihlar 1998; Shannon and Beach 1995).

Whatever the argument, the minimum wage changes may not affect child poverty rates in a significant manner. In 2003, out of over half a million minimum wage earners in Canada, two-thirds were women and one-quarter were part of couples (Sussman and Tabi 2004). That means that among couples, three-quarters of spouses were earning more than minimum wage. The other quarter in part reflects women who take lower-paying part-time jobs while raising young children. Among minimum wage earners, there were 27,000 single parents working at or below the minimum wage (Sussman and Tabi 2004). It is this group that is of particular interest for child poverty. Minimum wage earners are discussed in greater detail in Chapter 6, on the working poor. The impact of minimum wage rates on child poverty may not be as great as that of other factors.

Social inequality versus social spending argument

There is an argument in the social exclusion paradigm that growing inequality threatens the social inclusion of marginalized groups in a society. A Campaign2000 report from 2005 contends that Canada's failure to address child poverty is reflected in growing income inequality. It shows that social inequality has widened between 1993 and 2003. In 1993, the richest families earned 10 times more than the poorest families, whereas in 2003 they earned 13 times more (Campaign2000 2005). The increase in inequality may not be as large in terms of constant dollars. What could be more threatening to the social fibre is the marginalization of the poor. Many poor families are lone parents, recent immigrants, visible minorities, Aboriginal peoples, and persons with disabilities. The increased economic inequality tinged with social exclusion based on demographic or ethnic characteristics can lead to intergenerational poverty, making children its prime victims. The increased inequality erodes social cohesion, increases insecurity, and reduces public health (Jarjoura, Triplett, and Brinkler 2002).

Social spending seems to be a much better predictor of child poverty. The United Nations Children's Fund (UNICEF) reported in 2005 that every country among Organisation for Economic Co-operation and Development (OECD) countries that spent 10 percent of its national income on social spending had a child poverty rate below 10 percent. The United Kingdom had reached its interim target of a 25 percent reduction in child poverty by 2005 by increasing its social spending to meet its commitment of halving its child poverty rate by 2010 (UNICEF 2005). Canada devoted a little over 5 percent of its national income on social spending and ranked 19th among 26 OECD countries in a global survey of child poverty rates in industrialized countries (UNICEF 2005). Canada's success in reducing poverty rates among the elderly through government policies confirms that child poverty rates could also be reduced by increasing social spending.

Vulnerable children

Minority children are especially vulnerable to poverty. The rate of poverty is very high among these children as compared with other children.

Aboriginal children

Though we have discussed Aboriginal poverty in general in Chapter 2, on ethnic poverty, it is essential to consider Aboriginal children as a special case. Poverty among off-reserve children with at least one Aboriginal parent was 41 percent in 2001, which is 2.5 times the rate for Canada as a whole (Statistics Canada 2003a). The reason for this much higher rate is that Aboriginal workers earn two-thirds of an average Canadian worker's wage (Freiler, Rothman, and Barata 2004). There is a need for special programs for Aboriginal workers.

Children with disabilities

Child poverty among children with disabilities under 14 years of age was about 25 percent, compared with 19 percent for all children in the same age group (Statistics Canada 2003b). Children with disabilities are more likely to live in poor families because of financial stresses on the household related to the child's disability and due to household earnings lost when parents of children with disabilities have to leave the workforce to look after their disabled children (Freiler, Rothman, and Barata 2004).

Children from recent immigrant families

Another vulnerable group is recent immigrants. The poverty rate among recent immigrant families increased from about 25 percent in 1980 to around 39 percent in 2001 (Lochhead 2003). Low wages and barriers to employment due to non-recognition of credentials were the two major reasons for the increase in poverty among recent immigrant families. Yalnizyan (2000) reports that one-third of immigrants worked in low-wage sales and service occupations, and that new immigrants earned only 78 percent of the earnings of non-immigrant Canadians. This phenomenon of persistence of poverty among recent immigrants is fairly new. Historically, earnings of immigrants caught up with those of the Canadian-born within 10 years, but the economic downturn of the early 1990s had a serious impact on the earnings of new immigrants and their access to employment (Freiler, Rothman, and Barata 2004). Another change that has marked recent immigrants' economic experience in Canada is that their labour force participation rate has declined in the 1990s compared with earlier decades, when the labour force participation rate of immigrants was higher than that of Canadian-born workers. In 1991, the labour force participation rate for immigrants was about 69 percent, compared with 78 percent for Canadian adults overall. This gap has widened for recent immigrant women (McIsaac 2003).

Conceptual Explanation

Poverty segregates its victims from mainstream society both socially and psychologically. The isolation starts early among children who grow up in poor households. The chapter entitled "Are Poor Kids Bad Kids" in the report of the National Council of Welfare (1975) explains poor children's exclusion through the Protestant work ethic, which holds that monetary reward must be earned by hard work and that those who have nothing must deserve nothing. This belief among children is likely to create an association of being poor with being bad or being punished. When a poor child in school is left out of class outings and other extra-curricular activities, that child is likely to reason that he or she deserves this exclusion.

Adolescence reinforces the exclusion of a child. It is the time in children's development when they seek peer group approval to deal with the insecurities faced in the transition from childhood to adulthood. The isolation from the peer group makes an adolescent a target of ridicule, cruel pranks, taunts, and absurd jokes. An adolescent in this situation resolves the issue either by letting the ridicule continue or by forbidding the peers from engaging in such behaviour by being tough. Whether he or she remains helpless or assumes a tough posture, both strategies result in further behavioural problems; helplessness shatters self-confidence and being tough reshapes a poor child's self-image to fit a role that can be labelled delinquent.

A number of studies on understanding poverty discussed in Chapter 1 underline that there is a correlation between poverty and adolescent delinquency. Poor children have to get by with what they have got. They learn to beat the system or to be street smart at an early age—to get onto a bus or into a theatre without a ticket is not a game but a necessity.

Poverty generates insecurity in the family unit as a whole. Insecurities—such as being uncertain if next month's rent can be paid, if groceries will last till the welfare cheque arrives, and if the taxi money to take a sick child to the doctor will be available—do affect a young child adversely. The charity that serves a function of altruism for those who give out of well-meaning generosity becomes a source of stigma and shame for a child whose parents must accept it or be without food or clothing. When a poor child gets to a charity camp, he or she knows it, and the very knowledge is devastating.

Poverty helps to segregate poor children from mainstream society. When a poor child is left out of class outings and extracurricular activities, he or she thinks either that he or she is being punished or that his or her parents cannot afford the cost of participation. In adolescence, poverty isolates the child from the peer group. In school, where the stigma of poverty manifests for the first time, poor children again learn to beat the system by becoming street smart. The lack of recreation facilities and isolation from the peer group may result in delinquent activities. The delinquency marks the beginning of a prolonged isolation from rest of the society. This isolation from the potential source of income sets the stage for intergenerational poverty and possibility for the development of the culture of poverty.

In conclusion, all four concepts namely, the culture of poverty, the stigma of poverty, the situation perspective, and social exclusion, can be used to explain child poverty. This shows that child poverty is a complex issue. A multi-pronged and prolonged strategy that removes the stigma of poverty, alters adverse conditions that impede labour force participant of poor parents, and enhances inclusion of poor children and their parents in society is essential to develop programs to alleviate, if not fully eradicate, child poverty in society.

Chapter 6

The Working Poor

Introduction

A job is the best protection against poverty, yet for many Canadians paid work does not lift them above the poverty threshold. Why do a large number of people with earnings from work as a major source of their total income remain poor? The relationship between poverty and paid work requires some exploration. The limitations of work as protection against poverty can be understood by looking at the patterns of work of the low-wage poor or "working poor." The working poor are defined as individuals under the age of 65, and families with no family member aged 65 and over, whose income is below Statistics Canada's low income cut-offs (LICOs), and who earned more than half of that income from wages and salaries or from self-employment (National Council of Welfare 1981). In summary, the poor who obtain more than half of their income from employment are termed *the working poor,* those who earn less than half of their income from employment are termed *the other poor,* and those with incomes above the poverty line are termed *the non-poor.*

The importance of paid work as protection against poverty is best demonstrated by looking at workers by types of families with no member over 65 years of age. The common types of families are unattached men, unattached women, couples without children, two-parent families, and female single parents. Table 6-1 shows that about 6 in every 10 unattached poor persons, poor couples without children, and two-parent poor families are working poor. Even among poor single mothers who are constrained by their children, 1 in 4 are working poor. The employment income is called earnings. The earnings form the bulk of total income of the working poor—89 percent of income of unattached individuals,

Table 6-1   Poor Families and Unattached Individuals under 65 with Half or More of Their Income from Earnings, 2003

	Unattached Men	Unattached Women	Couples without Children	Two-Parent Families	Single-Parent Mothers
Number of Poor	540,000	474,000	152,000	240,000	287,000
Number of Working Poor	302,000	281,000	88,000	165,000	59,000
Percent of Working Poor	56	59	58	57	25
Average Annual Earnings	$8,804	$9,219	$10,945	$20,080	$14,074
Average Income from Other Sources	$1,100	$1,163	$2,565	$7,648	$7,260
Average Total Income	$9,904	$10,382	$13,510	$27,728	$21,334
Earnings as Percentage of Total Income	89	89	81	72	66

Source: National Council of Welfare. 2008. *Poverty Profile 2002 and 2003*. Ottawa: National Council of Welfare, Table 7.2.

81 percent of income of couples without children, 72 percent of income of two-parent families, and 66 percent of income of single parents (Table 6-1). This debunks the myth that poor do not work. According to Fleury and Fortin (2006), the working poor in Canada work, on average, as many hours as other workers (around 2,000 hours in a year). This proves that another common myth, that the poor do not work hard, is also incorrect. The main reason behind workers' poverty is that most of them work part-time, part of the year, for an unsteady number of hours (Fleury and Fortin 2006).

According to Fleury and Fortin (2006), almost 1 in every 10 working-age Canadians live in poverty, and over half of the total Canadian poor are working poor. The working poor form an unnoticed group of poor Canadians because those who work are not considered poor by society.

There is a lack of systematic research on the working poor in Canada. A National Council of Welfare report on the working poor written with the intention of filling the data gap found that the number of working poor families declined steadily between 1973 and 1977 (National Council of Welfare 1981). In the 1970s, the working poor were highly urbanized. They were more likely to work in service, sales, farming, fishing, or clerical

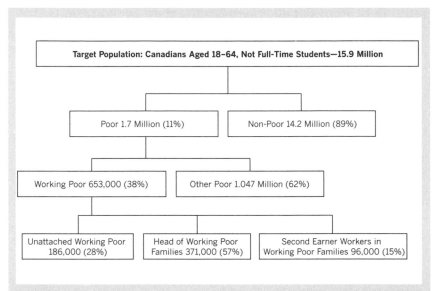

Figure 6-1   Number of Low-Income Individuals and Number of Working Poor Persons among All Individuals Aged 18-64 Who Were Not Full-Time Students in 2001

Source: Adapted from data in Fleury, Dominique, and Myriam Fortin. 2006. *When Working Is Not Enough to Escape Poverty: An Analysis of Canada's Poor*. Ottawa: Human Resources and Social Development Canada, 18. Available online.

jobs, and they were less likely to be employed full-year, although few received income from social assistance (National Council of Welfare 1981). Working poor families were also much more likely than other families to depend on only one earner. A majority of working poor Canadians were unattached individuals.

The National Council of Welfare updated the profile of working poor Canadians in subsequent Poverty Profile publications. According to these profiles, the proportion of low-income families in the working poor labour force (that is, either working or actively looking for work) remained virtually unchanged: 55 percent in 1969, 56 percent in 1986, and 59 percent in 2001. In 2000, the Canadian Council on Social Development (CCSD) also prepared a profile of working poor families, using a different definition. Their findings were quite similar to those of the National Council of Welfare. Out of about 16 million working-age Canadians, 1.7 million were poor, and among these poor, 653,000, or 38 percent, were the working poor. Among these working poor Canadians, 28 percent were unattached individuals, 57 percent were heads of families, and the remaining 15 percent were second earner workers in working poor families (Figure 6-1).

Profile of the Working Poor

Demographic characteristics

Table 6-2 reveals that the working poor were more likely to be men in their mid-thirties to mid-forties from the province of Ontario (with 34 percent working poor). Overall, 1 in every 9 working poor was a recent immigrant, or was an Aboriginal living off-reserve, or had work limitations. According to Fleury and Fortin (2006) British Columbia had the second-highest proportion (23 percent) of working poor, whereas the Atlantic provinces had the lowest proportion (10 percent).

Among larger cities, the incidence of poverty among workers was highest in Vancouver, where about 10 percent of workers were poor, compared with Winnipeg, Montreal, and the Ottawa-Gatineau region, where around 3 percent of workers were poor (Fleury and Fortin 2006).

Types of families

The working poor are more likely to be unattached persons, two-earner families with at least one or two children, or couples without children (Table 6-3). These are the couples in early stages of family formation; therefore, their poverty is likely to be a contributing factor to child poverty in Canada. It means that financial help to working poor young parents is likely to ameliorate child poverty in Canada.

Education

Education is an important predictor of poverty. Strangely, the working poor are not very different from the working non-poor in the middle ranges of educational attainment. The main difference is at the lower and the upper end. About 20 percent of working poor have less than a high-school education, compared with about 12 percent of working non-poor. And about 11 percent of the working poor have a university education, compared with 20 percent of the working non-poor (Table 6-4). Both the working poor and the working non-poor are predominantly high-school diploma holders.

Fleury and Fortin (2006) reported that close to half of the working poor live in families where some of the working-age adults are not working or are working very few hours. They are likely to be young, and either students or adults with low education. Those working poor who are students and are studying in universities or colleges are temporarily poor. Their incomes remain under the poverty line because they work part-time and that work is too sporadic. Their apparent "poverty" is a sign of an investment in education that will profit them when they enter the regular labour force.

Table 6-2   Distribution of Working Poor and Working Non-Poor Individuals by Demographic Characteristics, 2001

	Working Poor		Working Non-Poor	
	Number	Percent	Number	Percent
All Individuals	653,300	100.0	10,934,100	100.0
Gender				
Male	369,100	56.5	6,090,300	55.7
Female	284,200	43.5	4,843,800	44.3
Age				
18–24	77,700	11.9	710,700	6.5
25–34	162,000	24.8	2,569,500	23.5
35–44	207,100	31.7	3,520,800	32.2
45–54	143,100	21.9	2,974,100	27.2
55–64	63,400	9.7	1,170,000	10.7
Province				
Atlantic Provinces (NL, PEI, NB, NS)	62,700	9.6	787,300	7.2
Quebec	99,300	15.2	2,580,500	23.6
Ontario	220,200	33.7	4,373,700	40.0
Manitoba, Saskatchewan, Alberta	120,200	18.4	1,880,700	17.2
BC	150,900	23.1	1,323,000	12.1

Table 6-2   Continued

	Working Poor		Working Non-Poor	
	Number	Percent	Number	Percent
Marital Status				
Single (never married)	183,600	28.1	2,219,600	20.3
In a union (married or not)	355,400	54.4	7,612,100	69.7
Separated, divorced, widowed	114,300	17.5	1,093,400	10.0
Immigrant or Aboriginal Living Off-Reserve				
Yes	75,100	11.5	579,500	5.3
No	508,300	77.8	9,523,600	87.1
Work Limitations				
Yes	75,800	11.6	677,900	6.2
No	577,500	88.4	10,256,200	93.8

Source: Fleury, Dominique, and Myriam Fortin. 2006. "Distribution of Working Poor and Working Non-Poor Individuals by Education Attainment, 2001." *When Working Is Not Enough to Escape Poverty: An Analysis of Canada's Poor*. Ottawa: Human Resources and Social Development Canada, 23. Available online.

Table 6-3   Distribution of Working Poor and Working Non-Poor Individuals by Family Characteristics, 2001

Family Type	Working Poor		Working Non-Poor	
	Number	Percent	Number	Percent
All Individuals	**653,300**	**100.0**	**10,934,000**	**100.0**
Unattached	185,500	28.4	1,508,900	13.8
Couple without children, one earner	31,400	4.8	295,200	2.7
Couple without children, two earners	74,500	11.4	3,586,400	32.8
Couple with one or two children, one earner	54,200	8.3	229,600	2.1
Couple with one or two children, two earners or more	105,800	16.2	3,083,400	28.2
Couple with three children or more, one earner	28,100	4.3	76,500	0.7
Couple with three children or more, two earners or more	58,100	8.9	349,900	3.2
Lone-Parent family	64,700	9.9	798,200	7.3
Other family type	51,000	7.8	1,005,900	9.2

Source: Fleury, Dominique, and Myriam Fortin. 2006. "Distribution of Working Poor and Working Non-Poor Individuals by Education Attainment, 2001." *When Working Is Not Enough to Escape Poverty: An Analysis of Canada's Poor.* Ottawa: Human Resources and Social Development Canada, 23. Available online.

Table 6-4   Distribution of Working Poor and Working Non-Poor Individuals by Education Attainment, 2001

	Working Poor		Working Non-Poor	
Highest Level of Education	**Number**	**Percent**	**Number**	**Percent**
Less than a High School Diploma	128,000	19.6	1,279,300	11.7
High School Diploma	169,200	25.9	2,591,400	23.7
More than a High School Diploma	197,900	30.3	3,892,600	35.6
University	73,200	11.2	2,197,800	20.1

Source: Fleury, Dominique, and Myriam Fortin. 2006. "Distribution of Working Poor and Working Non-Poor Individuals by Education Attainment, 2001." *When Working Is Not Enough to Escape Poverty: An Analysis of Canada's Poor*. Ottawa: Human Resources and Social Development Canada, 32. Available online.

However, the low-income status of those working poor who are over 25 years of age is not an issue of temporary poverty. The older working poor family heads tend to have lower educational levels; therefore, they are more likely to remain poor without adequate skill training to augment their earnings (Fleury and Fortin 2006).

Income and employment

In Canada, a typical working family receives income mainly from wages or salaries but also some from government transfer payments and investments. According to Chen (2005), 11 percent of the working poor as opposed to about 6 percent of the working non-poor report self-employment as a major source of their income. These working poor are small farmers, fishermen, small-store operators, and some artisans who work seasonally (Chen 2005). The Canadian economy has shifted from predominantly manufacturing to mostly services over the past 20 years. It is therefore natural that a large proportion (one-third) of the working poor report working in the sales and services sector and two-thirds of them report working for small businesses (Fleury and Fortin 2006). The concentration of working poor in low-paid service-based jobs is one reason for their poverty.

Money that eligible unemployed workers receive in Canada is called Employment Insurance. Eligibility is based on the number of weeks worked. In 2001, only about 13 percent of the working poor received at least one dollar in Employment Insurance benefits (Fleury and Fortin 2006). The working poor are usually very susceptible to unemployment because they lack job stability. But this job instability is also the reason for the smaller number of Employment Insurance recipients among the working poor, because they are less likely to accumulate the required number of weeks worked to qualify for Employment Insurance.

Factors behind Working Poverty

The consumer finances surveys of Statistics Canada provide "cross-sectional" data, which represent a series of snapshots over the years. They help to draw conclusions about the size and composition of various income groups. There is no way of knowing whether the working poor are the same people who were counted among the working poor during a previous year, or whether they have moved to non-poor or the other poor categories. We need so-called longitudinal surveys, that is, surveys that follow the same population over the years, to develop a comprehensive portrait of poverty and income inequality. While recognizing these limitations, the National Council of Welfare (1981) considers the following four factors important in relation to the working poor:

* unemployment;
* growth in two-earner families;
* government transfer payments; and
* major government programs.

Unemployment

As was mentioned earlier, the working poor are very susceptible to unemployment because they lack job stability. Rising unemployment erodes the value of earnings of the working poor. Rising unemployment reduces the share of their annual income obtained from employment and shifts them from the working poor to the other poor, making them dependent on non-employment sources such as Employment Insurance, family allowances, and social assistance benefits. Similarly, many high-income persons who experience unemployment drop down to the near-poor or the working poor categories. It is possible that as a result of prolonged unemployment some working poor fall below the poverty line and become part of the other poor group.

Rising unemployment has an adverse effect on the earnings of working poor families and probably shifts some of them into the other poor income group, since during a period of high unemployment a higher proportion of their income comes from Employment Insurance than from employment (National Council of Welfare 1981). As is shown in Chapter 7, on regional poverty, the correlation coefficient between unemployment rates and poverty rates from 1987 to 2006 among persons of working age (18–64) in Canada is 0.74. The square of this coefficient would mean that 55 percent of the variation in poverty rates within the working-age population can be explained by the unemployment rates alone. The unemployment rate is a powerful indicator of poverty, particularly in the working-age population. Unemployment not only increases the rates of poverty among the working poor, but also pushes the working poor to the realm of other poor, making them dependent on the welfare state.

Women traditionally experienced higher unemployment than men, particularly those women employed in low-wage occupations. For example, in 1981, the overall unemployment rate for women was 9.4 percent, but for those women working in low-paying occupations, such as services, it was 11.4 percent (National Council of Welfare 1981). Traditionally, the loss of women's jobs was a factor responsible for the shift of working poor families to the category of the other poor. This has changed during recent years. As mentioned in Chapter 4, on women in poverty, the 2009 downturn in the labour market affected women less than men because the male-dominated goods-producing industries, mainly manufacturing and construction, experienced high employment losses, whereas employment continued to grow in female-dominated service industries, such as health care, social services, educational services, finance, and insurance (Ferrao 1 April 2011). Therefore, during the recent economic slowdown, the loss of a man's job would be responsible for shifting working poor families to the category of the other poor. If this trend continues, men will be more likely to lose their jobs and a two-earner working poor family would be at risk of moving to the other poor category on account of loss of a job of male earner.

The welfare caseloads are also affected by rising unemployment. In a climate of high unemployment, more and more unemployed workers pursue fewer and fewer job openings. This places employable welfare recipients at a disadvantage because the stiff job competition makes it harder for them to leave welfare and find jobs. When unemployed workers exhaust their Employment Insurance benefits, they add to the welfare roll. During the recession of the early 1980s, the increase among welfare recipients was attributed to "unemployed employable" persons. According to an Interprovincial Task Force (1980), 28 percent of welfare cases fell in this category in Canada.

Growth in two-earner families

In 1965, only 3 out of every 10 Canadian workers were women, whereas now almost 1 in 2 workers is a female (Human Resources and Skills Development Canada [HRSDC] 2005). In 1965, only one-quarter of mothers with children under the age of six were in the labour force, compared with over 70 percent at the end of 20th century (HRSDC 2005). The fertility rate also declined steadily, from 2.3 live births per woman in 1970 to 1.5 in 2000 (Statistics Canada 22 August 2011).

According to the Economic Council of Canada (1976), the growth in two-earner families is a key cause of the steady decline in working poverty. The addition of another breadwinner lifts the family into the near-poor or non-poor category. A second income acts as a cushion to absorb the shock if the other earner becomes unemployed. In 2001, only about 37 percent of working poor families had two or more earners, as compared with about 64 percent of the working non-poor families (Table 6-3). Also, the data show an increasing trend in the percentage of multiple earners among non-poor families. Families with multiple earners are also not completely immune to poverty. If both spouses in a family with children to support are low-wage earners, even a short bout of unemployment on the part of one of the spouses can push the family below the poverty line.

Government transfer payments

The Economic Council of Canada (1976) considered the "enriched social security system" a major cause of the decline in the number of working poor families and individuals in the early 1970s, whereas the National Council of Welfare (1981) contended that government security programs are hardly the ticket out of poverty. In spite of the divergent views of these agencies, the importance of government programs to family income in Canada cannot be ignored. These programs include family allowance, public pensions, Employment Insurance, worker's compensation, tax exemptions and deductions, old age security income, and social assistance. Though public transfers are an important part of the income of all families and unattached individuals, they are particularly important to lower-income families. In 2001, 90 percent of the working poor had at least one dollar of income from government transfer payments, compared with 45 percent of the working non-poor. One-quarter of the income of the working poor was in the form of government transfers, compared with less than 5 percent of that of the working non-poor Canadians (Fleury and Fortin 2006).

Government benefits are extremely important for the working poor because generous government transfer payments can help shift some families into a higher income category and consequently, can induce a decline in the number of the working poor. Ironically, the growth of government transfer payments can increase the number of other poor while at the same time reducing the number of working poor. This is because the working poor are defined as those who obtain half or more of their (low) income from work. If a family obtains just over half of its income from generous government payments, then these payments can alter the balance of sources of income and can shift the working poor family into the category of the other poor. The family allowance in Canada increased substantially during the 1970s. According to the National Council of Welfare (1981), an enriched family allowance could close the gap between family income and the poverty line only for families with two children, not for families with more or fewer than two children. This is because the amount of family allowance for one child tends to be smaller and does not increase income enough to go over the poverty line of one-child families; and the poverty line increases for families with more than two children so much that family allowance payments do not increase income enough to go above the increased poverty line for these families. It was this conclusion that led the National Council of Welfare to assume that government security programs are not the solution to poverty for the working poor.

Minimum wages

Most Canadians working in private industry and for the federal, provincial, and municipal governments are protected by minimum wage laws. The minimum wage for students and young workers is lower than the general minimum wage in most provinces. An employee working full-time, full year on minimum wage will earn around 40 percent of an average wage (Table 6-5). The minimum wage does not provide absolute protection against poverty; however, it does ensure that low-paid workers do not fall below a specified floor of earnings and are not exploited by unscrupulous employers.

Usually minimum wages are sufficient to lift single persons above the poverty line, but not families. The distance between minimum wage income and the poverty line increases with the increase in the size of the family. The larger families receive more income from family allowance, child tax credits, other tax rebates, and income supplements. These transfer payments may not lift some larger families with minimum wage earnings above the poverty line. In other words, it does not mean that minimum wages are responsible for the working family poverty. The average minimum wage earners do not have to support a family; they are either young single persons living alone or married women who supplement

Table 6-5   Minimum Wage, Provinces, Territories, and Canada, 2008

	Minimum Wage	Minimum Wage as Percentage of Average Wage
Newfoundland and Labrador	$8.50	43
Prince Edward Island	$8.00	45
New Brunswick	$7.75	42
Nova Scotia	$8.10	43
Quebec	$8.50	41
Ontario	$8.75	39
Manitoba	$8.50	44
Saskatchewan	$8.60	41
Alberta	$8.40	34
British Columbia	$8.00	36
Northwest Territories	$8.25	35
Nunavut	$10.00	46
Yukon	$8.85	41
Canada	$8.14	37

Sources: Human Resources and Skills Development Canada. n.d. "Hourly Minimum Wages in Canada for Adult Workers." *Labour*. Ottawa: Human Resources and Skills Development Canada. Last modified 2 March 2012. Available online; Statistics Canada. n.d. *Average Hourly Wages of Employees by Selected Characteristics and Profession, Unadjusted Data, by Province (Monthly)*. Available online.
Note: Minimum wage is as of 1 January 2009.

their husbands' earnings by their wages. In this sense, an adequate minimum wage could provide a cushion against poverty to single persons and to some smaller families.

According to Fleury and Fortin (2006), fewer than 7 percent of the salaried working poor compared with less than 2 percent of the salaried working non-poor earned the minimum wage. This indicates that working poor Canadians are more likely than their working non-poor counterparts to earn minimum wage. Their data show that of the 653,000 working poor, 186,000 (28 percent) were unattached individuals (Figure 6-1). Most of the unattached working poor do not work enough hours in a year to bring their income above the poverty line (National Council of Welfare 1981). Therefore the minimum wage is an ineffectual remedy for reducing poverty among the working poor. Young workers often work at or slightly above the minimum wage and face a high level of unemployment. The unemployment rate of 5.1 percent in 2007 among Canadians 25 to 54 years old was the lowest it had been in the past 30 years; the unemployment rate of 11.2 percent for youth, despite dropping to its lowest in 1989, remained the highest among all the age groups (Statistics Canada 2008).

A short bout of unemployment for minimum wage earners can push them below the poverty line. The minimum wages tend to be inadequate and an unrealistic cure for the income problems of the working poor because the majority of working poor work less than year-round and the self-employed working poor are not included in minimum wage legislations. But the gap between minimum wage earnings and average earnings is an important indicator of working poverty. The Special Senate Committee as far back as 1971 suggested that the minimum wage should be increased regularly to maintain a rate equal to 60 percent of the average wage. Yet, numbers in Table 6-5 reveal that even almost 40 years later, despite this recommendation, minimum wage workers in Canada earn between 34 and 47 percent of the average wage.

Social programs and working poverty

Although federal programs, such as the National Child Benefit, Employment Insurance, social assistance, the minimum wage, and various provincial programs benefit the working poor directly or indirectly, few of these programs are specifically targeted at the working poor. The main findings of a major study on the working poor conducted by Fleury and Fortin (2006) based on Statistics Canada's Survey of Labour and Income Dynamics (SLID) data can be summarized as follows:

The poverty rate is an indication of the percentage of population that is poor. It does not measure the depth of poverty. The depth of poverty is measured by the poverty gap; that is, the amount of money required to bring the poor to the level of the poverty line. Surprisingly, the depth of poverty for unattached working poor individuals and for the heads of working poor families on average was not statistically different from the poverty depth of the non-working poor (Fleury and Fortin 2006). This means that poverty is no less severe for the working poor.

Another important point that Fleury and Fortin's (2006) study made is that the working poor have a strong attachment to the labour market. They worked, on average, as many hours as non-poor workers. The working poor faced less favourable conditions and inequitable access to employment-related benefits. Those who worked for a salary were more likely to have an atypical schedule and earned on average two-thirds of the hourly wage of other workers. As mentioned earlier, only a small proportion of the working poor earned a minimum wage, which indicates that increasing the minimum wage will have only a limited impact on their poverty.

According to Fleury and Fortin (2006), government support is more important in reducing working poverty. They assert that the working poor are more likely to use social assistance and less likely to use Employment Insurance because a large proportion of the working poor are self-employed and would thus not be eligible for Employment Insurance. A contributory program similar to Employment Insurance for self-employed individuals may help to reduce working poverty, although the under-reporting of income by those working poor who work for cash will be a major impediment in implementing such a program. The self-employed working poor report working longer hours than their salaried counterparts yet remain poor. There may be over-reporting of working poverty among the self-employed because many self-employed persons with small business may work for cash and may under-report their real income (Fleury and Fortin 2006). The self-employed also tend to be eligible for more tax-deductions than the other poor.

A working family with a sole earner is more likely to be poor. Workers with many dependent children are also more likely to be poor—whether or not they are sole earner in the family. Sole bread-winners and those with many dependent children with a modest income are more likely to be poor. Although low hourly wages may increase working poverty, they are not the most important determinant. The more significant determinants of working poverty are being a sole earner in the family and having many dependent children (Fleury and Fortin 2006). Being an older worker (45–59 years) is also a factor, as are not working full-time full year, working for a small business, and working in the sales and service industry (Fleury and Fortin 2006).

Initiatives to Ameliorate Working Poverty

There are some other policy initiatives that can help ameliorate working poverty. Research shows that the working poor experience fluctuations in the number of work hours available during the year (Fleury, Fortin, and Luong 2005; Fortin and Fleury 2006). Therefore, policies encouraging employment stability will improve the plight of the working poor. Those policies that encourage creation of full-time full year jobs rather than part-time employment are more likely to help the working poor.

We have seen earlier that it is the structure of the economic family—being the sole earner or having many children—that gets in the way of the working poor's earnings. The policies could be targeted to entice the second earner in the working poor family to work. Providing assistance to purchase child care would relieve the second earners from family responsibilities and encourage them to join the labour market. Assistance to avail oneself of flexible child care may be more beneficial to a low-income worker than a non-refundable tax benefit because the working poor pay very little income tax. At the same time, a large number of the working poor are unattached. These workers will not benefit from child care assistance. They may require a supplement to their earned income to become non-poor. Similarly, the high-risk working poor, such as Aboriginal peoples living off-reserve or recent immigrants, may benefit from government financial incentives to employers to hire these individuals.

The attachment to the labour market of the working poor is no different than that of the working non-poor; they just experience higher levels of unemployment or underemployment, or reduced number of hours of paid work (Fleury, Fortin, and Luong 2005; Fleury and Fortin 2006). For this reason, eligibility for financial assistance should be determined based on the working poor person's work history of several years because a single year of work history may not identify the target population.

Fleury, Fortin, and Luong (2005) analyzed the spending patterns of working families and recommend that better access to affordable housing, supplementary health care, and transport subsidies will benefit the working poor and help ameliorate working poverty. A benefit to working poor families could be delivered through the tax system that provides family-income-tested benefits tied to earnings.

Conceptual Explanation

The notion of the culture of poverty does not apply to working poverty. First, we do not see traits such as low level of organization, overcrowding, gregariousness, unprotected childhood, female-headed households, and mother-centred families. Second, the culture of poverty implies that just like culture, the culture of poverty also has rural and urban differences. But working poverty is by and large an urban phenomenon. A large proportion of working poor are students and recent immigrants who experience poverty for a relatively short time. The term *the culture of poverty* entails poverty that is a long-lasting condition; therefore, it will not be applicable to these working poor. Finally, because the working poor have a similar profile to their non-poor counterparts, they are unlikely to constitute a distinct culture of poverty.

The argument that poverty is a group stigma that results in the social and economic isolation of the poor also does not seem to apply to working poverty. The stigma of poverty argument insists that poverty will persist as long as stigma persists. We know that as soon as work conditions change to bring adequate income to the working poor, they escape poverty.

Both the situational perspective and the concept of social exclusion are, however, helpful to explain working poverty. The situational perspective asserts that the poor behave differently not because they possess a unique value system; rather, they accept middle-class values but lack the means to realize them. Programs that enhance income can change the situation for the working poor. When individuals are unable to participate in any of the key economic, social, and political activities, they suffer exclusion from those social networks that provide access to such social commodities as employment, housing, education, income, status, and power. This idea of social exclusion can be useful to explain working poverty. In fact, policies that seek to ameliorate working poverty try to make social commodities more accessible to the poor. The policies that promote inclusion of low-income workers in the social and economic institutions would be ideal to tackle working poverty in a society.

Chapter 7

Regional Poverty in Canada

Introduction

Poverty in Canada cannot be viewed as a social problem that is just endemic to certain groups living within particular neighbourhoods of urban areas, such as Jane and Finch in Toronto or the Downtown Eastside in Vancouver. A major issue in this country is the continued existence of an entire region, such as the Atlantic provinces, whose economic development lags behind that of the nation as a whole.

Regional differences are closely associated with its local economy. For example, poverty rates tend to fluctuate with the state of the provincial economy. Table 7-1 shows how ranking of provinces on poverty rates changed during recession and recovery periods over the last three decades. Historically, Ontario and Newfoundland were at opposite ends of the poverty spectrum. The recession of 1982 changed this picture, when the poverty rates of Quebec, Manitoba, Nova Scotia, and New Brunswick rose above the rate of Newfoundland. It changed again during the 1989 economic recovery, when the four Western provinces had poverty rates above the national average. And a profound change took place in 1999, when British Columbia, whose resource economy was affected by the economic downturn, replaced Newfoundland as the province having the highest poverty rate in the country. Until the 2008 downturn, the poverty rates in Quebec and Manitoba had been above the national average. The economic downturn of 2008 affected Ontario the most and in 2009, Ontario's poverty rate exceeded the national average for the first time. Ontario's economy, particularly the manufacturing sector, is integrated with that of the United States. The US economic downturn affected Ontario's exports and employment, resulting in an increase in poverty in Ontario.

In this chapter, we will discuss regional differences in terms of provincial differences. Though provinces are not necessarily homogeneous economic

Table 7-1 Poverty Rates by Province, Selected Years

Province	1982	1983	1989	1992	1993	1996	1999	2002	2008	2009
Newfoundland and Labrador	**14.9**	**20.2**	**10.3**	**15.8**	13.9	**15.4**	**14.3**	**11.4**	7.3	7.0
Prince Edward Island	10.7	9.2	6.6	7.2	5.8	8.6	9.5	7.3	5.2	4.8
Nova Scotia	**12.5**	12.2	9.9	11.0	12.3	13.4	11.4	9.9	8.3	8.0
New Brunswick	**15.1**	**18.2**	**10.3**	11.8	12.4	12.0	10.3	9.8	7.1	6.7
Quebec	**15.0**	**15.9**	**12.3**	**14.8**	**17.4**	**18.0**	**14.8**	**12.3**	**11.2**	9.4
Ontario	10.9	12.8	7.8	10.8	12.0	14.0	11.3	10.7	9.3	**10.1**
Manitoba	**15.5**	13.7	**12.4**	**16.1**	**15.6**	**15.8**	**14.9**	**12.2**	8.6	8.9
Saskatchewan	11.0	12.0	**11.8**	**14.3**	**14.8**	13.0	10.2	8.6	7.2	7.0
Alberta	9.1	13.1	**12.4**	**17.1**	**14.7**	14.8	11.8	9.4	5.6	7.7
British Columbia	12.1	13.5	**10.4**	**14.2**	13.8	**15.2**	**16.4**	**16.0**	**11.4**	**12.0**
Canada	**12.4**	**14.0**	**10.2**	**13.3**	**14.1**	**15.2**	**13.0**	**11.6**	**9.4**	**9.6**

Source: Statistics Canada. 2010b. "Tables 202-0802 and 202-0804." *Income in Canada*. Statistics Canada Catalogue no. 75-202-X. Ottawa: Statistics Canada.
Note: Provincial numbers in bold indicate equal to or above the national average rate.

Table 7-2   Urban Population in Canada as Percentage of Total Population, Selected Years

1950	1960	1970	1980	1990	2000	2005	2015	2030
60.8	68.9	75.7	75.7	76.6	79.4	81.1	84.0*	87.2*

Source: United Nations Statistics Division. 2006. "Urban Population." Globalis 2006 Indicator. Available online.
*forecast

regions, their independent geopolitical status is a sufficient reason to consider them as regions. The problems of regional disparities, which result in unequal distributions of poverty across Canada, have their roots in such economic factors as urbanization, employment levels, inflation, the uneven distribution of income, the dependence of the region on some particular industry or economic activity, the depopulation of certain areas, and the fear of overcrowding of others (Brewis 1970).

Urbanization

Rapid growth in the 20th century in Western nations has been a result of industrialization. Between 1900 and 2000, Canada's economy grew 25-fold. An industrial economy was at its incubation stage at the time of confederation in 1867, when half of the nation's labour force worked in the primary sectors (agriculture, mining, forestry, and fishing) of the economy. In fact, one-half of the nation's income was generated from this sector. Today less than 10 percent of the labour force is employed in the primary industries. Industrialization required an urbanized population for markets as well as a labour supply. In 1871, only 18 percent of Canada was urban, but by 2005 more than 81 percent of Canadians lived in urbanized areas. It is projected that by 2030, 9 out of every 10 Canadians will live in urban areas (Table 7-2).

Many changes in Canadian society were brought on by the urban-industrialized systems that are responsible for today's regional disparities. Family size shrank and familial ties weakened as nuclear families replaced the joint family system. The nature of work radically changed from autonomous, unskilled, and irregular work in the agriculture sector to controlled, skilled, and organized work in the industrial economy.

The urban economy places a premium on training. Workers in an urbanized society often need to retrain themselves to adjust to rapid technological changes. Moreover, in an urbanized-industrialized society, workers must be highly mobile—geographically as well as occupationally. In addition, they must be sufficiently young, so that the employer's investment in their training can be fully repaid.

The implications of these changes are that the older workers in an urban setting come to bear the brunt of technological changes. Even at the age of 50, employers start assuming that the period of investment in employees' training is too small, and the workers become technologically redundant. It is no wonder that unemployed older workers find it far more difficult to regain employment than do younger workers. The elderly are also not immune to the changes brought about by urbanization. As economic prosperity leads to an increase in life expectancy, the span of unproductive retired life also increases. In the absence of adequate savings and public transfer payments (pensions, etc.), the elderly become a major part of the urban poor. Although Canada has been fairly successful in implementing policies to ameliorate elderly poverty (including the abolishment of a mandatory retirement age in several provinces) and their poverty rate is low and has remained unchanged for the past few years (from 2006 to 2009) (Statistics Canada 2010), the elderly still remain vulnerable to poverty. Though poverty has declined among the elderly in general, the gap between poverty rates of male and female elderly still remains high; elderly women, and particularly unattached elderly women, have higher rates of poverty than do elderly men.

Urbanization also brings problems for younger women. In urban settings, single mothers' geographical and occupation mobility is hindered if adequate daycare services are not available for their young children. Often these mothers cannot rely on the help of extended families for daycare service for their children. The presence of children and the lack of daycare services make single parents immobile, and this immobility makes them prime candidates for poverty. Urban ethnic people, such as black people in the United States and First Nations people in urban Canada, remain segregated from their respective mainstream societies. Assuming that increased urbanization will continue to bring increased urban poverty, we can conclude from the projected figures of urbanization in Canada (Table 7-2) that in the future 9 of out of every 10 poor Canadians will live in cities.

Rural Poverty

Urbanization also affects the rural population. Industrialization and mechanization increase demand for the secondary (production of goods) and the tertiary (distribution of goods and services) industries, and also increase production of the primary industries. This causes a decline in the demand for rural labour. In the rural economy, unlike in the urban economy, alternative employment opportunities are few. Thus rural poverty tends to be general, not confined to certain groups. In Canada, the regions where a major portion of the labour force is employed in the primary industries (fishing, agriculture, mining, and forestry) tend to have high incidence of poverty. Rural Canadians, comprising at least 20 percent of Canada's population, tend to have less access to health services and live in poorer conditions than their urban counterparts. The following excerpt describes the struggle of a family against poverty in rural New Brunswick:

> Dipping water from a spring in the ground, crouching in the wretched leanto that serves as a toilet, or trying to block the cracks around the windows in the midst of a frigid . . . winter. The Fisher family knows first-hand the rigors of rural poverty . . . housing conditions comparable to those in the Third World. . . .
> The Fishers, and their two sons . . . are trapped by poverty. . . .
> The front to their house is clad in black, tarry siding boards. . . . Call it what you will. Tentest . . . tar-soaked cardboard. . . . Inside, about one-third of the floor space has been partitioned off into rooms for the two boys. . . .
> Ten years ago, the Fishers tried to get a fresh start in Alberta during the oil boom. That was just after their youngest boy had died of leukemia. . . . It didn't work out. . . .
> They moved back . . . into their present dwelling . . . have occasionally found work during the potato harvest, but nothing steady. (Spears 1989)

Regions in Canada vary in the rural and urban composition—half of the population of the Atlantic provinces lives in rural areas, whereas less than 20 percent of the population of Quebec, Ontario, Alberta, and British Columbia live in rural areas. This rural–urban regional disparity is likely to cause differences in the prevalence and nature of poverty in various regions.

Regional Disparities

There is a wide range of literature on the existence of economic regional disparities in Canada (McInnis 1968; Green 1971; Economic Council of Canada 1977) and on the policies to redress these disparities (Lithwick 1978; Munro 1978; Weaver and Gunton 1982). It is interesting to note that scholars believe that regional inequality in Canada has not changed significantly since the 1940s, when the issue first became an important policy debate (Mansell and Copithorne 1986). Regional disparities in unemployment, inflation, income, and demographic factors are important determinants of regional poverty. Table 7-3 provides data on five important factors of provincial disparity:

Table 7-3   Factors Associated with Regional Disparity, by Region

Region	Personal Disposable Income (2002)	Unemployment Rate (2011)	Percent Population Urban (2006)	Consumer Price Index (CPI) (2008) 2002=100	Net Migration (1991–2006) in 1,000s
Newfoundland and Labrador	18,274	**12.7**	58	**114.3**	-71.3
Prince Edward Island	18,956	**11.3**	55	**117.5**	2.3
Nova Scotia	20,123	**8.8**	56	**115.9**	-20.0
New Brunswick	19,189	**9.5**	51	113.2	-20.6
Quebec	20,662	**7.8**	**80**	112.7	-140.4
Ontario	**23,692**	**7.8**	**85**	113.3	-4.9
Manitoba	20,739	5.4	72	113.4	-71.2
Saskatchewan	19,004	5.0	65	**115.9**	-88.6
Alberta	**25,539**	5.5	**82**	**121.6**	285.3
British Columbia	21,201	**7.5**	**85**	112.3	140.1
Canada	**22,268**	**7.4**	**80**	**114.1**	

Sources: Statistics Canada. 9 May 2007 (modified). *Per Capita Personal Disposable Income.* Ottawa: Statistics Canada. Available online.
Unemployment rate: Statistics Canada. 6 January 2012 (modified). "CANSIM Table 282-0002." *Labour Force, Employed and Unemployed, Numbers and Rates, by Province.* Available online.
CPI: Statistics Canada. 20 January 2012 (modified). "CANSIM Table 326-0021" and Statistics Canada Catalogue nos. 62-001-X and 62-010-X. Ottawa: Statistics Canada.
Net migration: Statistics Canada, Demography Division. 2008. *Canadian Demographics at a Glance.* Statistics Canada Catalogue no. 91-003-XWE. Ottawa: Statistics Canada.
Note: Provincial numbers in bold indicate equal or above the national average rate.

- personal disposable income;
- unemployment rate;
- percent population urban;
- cost of living (consumer price index); and
- net migration.

Regional income disparities

Personal disposable income is defined as the income that is left for households to spend after taxes and deductions for social security. While Ontario and Alberta in 2002 had personal disposable incomes above the national average, the disposable income of the Atlantic provinces, Manitoba, Saskatchewan, and British Columbia fell below the national average (Table 7-3). Regional variation in poverty is associated with regional disparity in personal disposable income, which in turn is associated with labour quality. According to Mansell and Copithorne (1986), 70 percent of the variation in per-worker earnings can be attributed to differences in labour quality. The quality of the labour force depends on its education, training, and health. A physically healthy workforce has low absenteeism, increased life expectancy, and higher productivity. Higher life expectancy prolongs the working life of workers, during which the economy reaps the benefit of the education and training that workers received during their younger years. Regional disparity in income creates a vicious circle for the quality of labour and for attracting industry to a region. The poorer regions lack the income that can be invested in the quality of labour, and industry is unlikely to locate in places where the quality of labour is not at a desirable level. This is reflected in the ranking of the provinces on personal disposable income (Table 7-3). The Atlantic provinces have disposable income below the national average, whereas disposable incomes of Ontario and Alberta are above the national average. Alberta has been able to attract energy-based industry and Ontario is the centre of the auto industry. Both these industries are capital intensive.

Regional differences in unemployment

Poverty rates are highly correlated with unemployment rates. The correlation coefficient between the poverty rate and the unemployment rate calculated from the data used in Figure 7-1 is 0.74, which means that about 55 percent of the variation in poverty rates can be explained by unemployment rates alone. Not only are there large regional variations in the extent of unemployment, but there is also a tendency for the lowest-income regions to have the highest unemployment rates over a business cycle (Mansell and

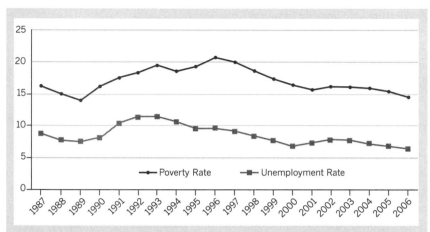

Figure 7-1 Unemployment Rate and Poverty Rate (All Persons), Canada, 1987–2006

Source: Poverty rates: Statistics Canada. 3 June 2009 (modified). "Table 1-1" *Income in Canada*. Statistics Canada Catalogue no. 75- 202-X. Ottawa: Statistics Canada. Unemployment rates: Newfoundland & Labrador Statistics Agency, Statistics Canada/Economics and Statistics Branch. 2009. *Labour Force Survey*. Available online.

Copithorne 1986). Newfoundland traditionally has low disposable income and a high unemployment rate, which are correlated with a higher poverty rate (Table 7-3).

Regional differences in inflation

Another unavoidable feature of a capitalist economy such as Canada's is the persistence of inflation. The value of the dollar continues to fall over time, and no region or sector of the economy is immune to this economic problem. Inflation varies from one region to another; it is usually high in the metropolitan areas where the urban poor live and in remote areas where the Aboriginal poor live. According to the Bank of Canada (2011), the value of dollar has been reduced by about 52 percent over the past 20 years. An item that cost one dollar in 1989 would cost $1.52 today, on average; it will be even higher in the metropolitan areas where the majority of Canada's poor live. Table 7-3 gives the values of the consumer price index for 2008 by province for all items. The province that has been hardest hit by inflation is Alberta, where prices have increased by almost 22 percent just within six years. The Atlantic provinces have a cost of living that is above the national average, which means the poor will have a harder time in these provinces.

Regional differences in demographic factors

The population of a region forms its employment base. Variations in unemployment rates, labour force participation rates, and population age structure account for over 40 percent of the post–World War II regional inequalities in per capita earned income in Canada (Mansell and Copithorne 1986). The regional differences in age structure can be due to differences in mortality, fertility, or migration. Though differences in mortality and fertility by province are converging in Canada, the gain and loss of population due to net migration is a significant factor in regional disparities.

The chronic persistence of lower incomes and higher unemployment in the Atlantic provinces and higher wage rates and incomes in central Canada can be expected to result in migration of labour from the former to the latter. At the time of the first Canadian census, in 1871, over 20 percent of the Canadian population lived in the three Atlantic provinces; by 1966, less than 7 percent did (Brewis 1970). The trend continues. Over the past 15 years, British Columbia and Alberta have seen big gains of migrants from other provinces, whereas the Atlantic provinces have lost population to other provinces (Table 7-3).

According to Brewis (1970), the decline in population reduces the incentive to produce for a local market because certain overhead costs still have to be borne by a smaller population. At the same time, out-migration consists largely of young adults and thus leaves a less favourable age structure for the economy to be vibrant in the place-of-origin of migrants. The low incomes and the traditional net loss of population due to migration in the Atlantic region seem to support Brewis's argument. In the larger provinces, such as Quebec and Ontario, the migration issue would not be as serious as it is for the smaller provinces, because it is usually easier to create employment opportunities in a larger population base.

Regional Poverty

The differentials in income, unemployment, urbanization, inflation, and interprovincial migration are not the only factors that affect regional disparity in Canada. Social (e.g., literacy, education, expenditure on social welfare), health (e.g., infant mortality, morbidity), and economic (e.g., income per capita, consumption per capita, employment) factors also play a role. The disparities in these indicators are likely to manifest themselves as different levels of regional incomes and employment opportunities, which in turn are likely to reflect differences in the levels of poverty. The following discussion of regional differences in the poverty rates of disadvantaged demographic groups is not meant to provide specific causes, but rather to show that because there are regional differences in the above-mentioned factors, regional differences in poverty are inevitable.

Regional differences in poverty among the elderly

Regional differences in the distribution of the elderly population across Canada are likely to influence regional differences in elderly poverty to some extent. The fertility decline that began in the mid-1960s and the steady increase in life expectancy in the 20th century contributed to almost uninterrupted aging of populations of all the provinces. This trend in population aging is expected to accelerate throughout the country; remember that the first baby boomers turned 65 in 2011.

The risk of poverty for the elderly varies according to the province in which they live (Table 7-4). According to before-tax rates, the elderly in Quebec are at the highest risk of poverty. Here almost 1 in every 5 elderly persons is poor. The incidence of poverty among the elderly in British Columbia, Manitoba, and Prince Edward Island is also higher than the national average. The elderly in the other six provinces have poverty rates lower than the national average. Alberta has the lowest rate, with only 7.8 percent of the elderly living in poverty. In recent years, economic growth

Table 7-4   Elderly Poverty by Province, 2004

Province	Elderly Poor	Percent of Elderly Poor	Before-Tax Poverty Rate[a]
Newfoundland and Labrador	8,000	1.5	13.3
Prince Edward Island	3,000	0.6	16.5
Nova Scotia	16,000	2.9	13.1
New Brunswick	13,000	2.4	13.9
Quebec	193,000	35.5	20.3
Ontario	166,000	30.6	11.1
Manitoba	24,000	4.4	16.3
Saskatchewan	16,000	2.9	12.2
Alberta	24,000	4.4	7.8
British Columbia	80,000	14.7	14.8
Canada (excluding Territories)	**543,000**	**100.0**	**14.0**

Source: National Council of Welfare. 2007. "Poverty among Seniors by Province, 2004." *Poverty Profile 2004*. Ottawa: National Council of Welfare. Available online.
[a]After-tax rates are better measures of poverty but could not be used in this table because they were unreliable for six provinces due to small sample size.

and in-migration of younger persons to Alberta from the other provinces of Canada due to the oil boom have helped Alberta's population to be relatively more prosperous and younger.

The correlation coefficient between the percentage of the elderly population and the elderly poverty rate by province is only 0.33. This means that the size of the elderly population is not a major predictor of provincial differences in poverty rates among the elderly. This is because not all provinces have provincial income security programs aimed at supplementing the incomes of the elderly, and the minimum guaranteed income provided to the elderly by the federal government is not always enough to protect the elderly from poverty. For example, the high rates of elderly poverty of Quebec and Prince Edward Island are a reflection of the absence of a provincial program targeted specifically to the elderly.

Regional differences in poverty among women

There are two factors that would explain the regional differences in poverty among women. They are the number of single female parents and the adequacy of welfare payments. Welfare income as a proportion of the poverty line for lone parents with one child is adequate only in Newfoundland and Labrador. For the other provinces, the proportion varies between 66 percent for Manitoba and 95 percent for Saskatchewan (Table 7-5). One of the reasons why welfare payments remain inadequate is that the rates are hiked every few years rather than being indexed to cost of living annually.

Regional differences in child poverty

The child poverty rate in Canada increased in the early 1980s and peaked at 15 percent in 1996. Since 1996, it has been on the decline, reaching a rate of about 10 percent in 2009 (Statistics Canada June 2011a). The distribution of these poor children by province is quite uneven. The child poverty rate in 2004 ranged from 4.6 percent in Prince Edward Island to 18.1 percent in British Columbia (Table 7-6). Ontario and Manitoba had child poverty rates similar to the national average. Only British Columbia and Newfoundland and Labrador had rates over the national average. British Columbia's child poverty rate was 41 percent higher than the national average, and Newfoundland's was 31 percent lower than the national average.

Regional differences in working poverty

We have seen in Chapter 6, on the working poor, that rates of poverty among workers have a very high correlation with unemployment rates.

Table 7-5   Total Welfare Income as Percentage of After-Tax Low Income Cut-Offs (LICOs) for Lone Parents with One Child and Couples with Two Children, 2009

Provinces and Territories	Lone Parent with One Child (%)	Couple with Two Children (%)
Newfoundland and Labrador	102	76
Prince Edward Island	88	83
Nova Scotia	79	71
New Brunswick	85	67
Quebec	78	65
Ontario	77	65
Manitoba	66	62
Saskatchewan	95	81
Alberta	78	70
British Columbia	75	61

Source: Adapted from National Council of Welfare. 2010. *Welfare Incomes 2009*. Ottawa: National Council of Welfare. Available online.

Table 7-6   Child Poverty Rate (defined as percent below low income cut-offs after tax), by Province, 2004

Province	Rate
Newfoundland and Labrador	**16.7**
Prince Edward Island	4.6
Nova Scotia	11.9
New Brunswick	8.8
Ontario	**12.8**
Quebec	10.9
Manitoba	**12.8**
Saskatchewan	10.9
Alberta	11.7
British Columbia	**18.1**
Canada (excluding Territories)	**12.8**

Source: National Council of Welfare. March 2007. "Child Poverty Rate (defined as percent below low income cut-offs after tax), by Province, 2004." *Poverty Profile 2004*. Ottawa: National Council of Welfare. Available online.
Note: Numbers in bold indicate equal to or above the national average rate.

Table 7-7 Percent of Working Poor by Province, 1980, 1990, and 2000

Province	1980	1990	2000	Percent Change from 1980 to 1990	Percent Change from 1990 to 2000
Newfoundland	10.1	8.3	10.3	-18	24
Prince Edward Island	12.9	9.1	10.2	-29	12
Nova Scotia	9.6	9.0	11.3	-6	26
New Brunswick	9.8	9.3	10.6	-5	14
Quebec	7.1	8.2	9.1	15	11
Ontario	6.7	6.4	7.3	-4	14
Manitoba	9.9	11.0	10.7	11	-3
Saskatchewan	11.1	14.5	12.7	31	-12
Alberta	7.3	9.9	8.8	36	-11
British Columbia	6.0	8.1	9.1	35	12
Yukon	6.4	6.4	7.9	0	23
NWT/Nunavut	11.4	10.3	9.5	-18	24

Source: Chen, Wen-Hao. 2005. *Examining the Working Poor in Canada: Is Working a Ticket Out of Poverty?* Ottawa: Statistics Canada, Table 3. Available online.

Unemployment is associated with economic activity; therefore, change in the rate of working poverty is associated with change in the economic conditions of the region. During the 1980s, the economy of the Atlantic provinces was much better than that of the Western provinces—Manitoba, Saskatchewan, and Alberta; therefore, working poverty rates declined in the Atlantic provinces and increased in the Western provinces. The reverse was true for these two regions in the 1990s. The economy of Manitoba, Saskatchewan, and Alberta was robust in 1990s and the proportion of the working poor declined (Table 7-7). But apart from the state of economy, as we have seen, programs targeted to the working poor also ameliorate working poverty. The minimum wage is one such program.

Miniumum wage and working poverty

There is a strong connection between low minimum wage and working poverty (Murray and Mackenzie 2007). The rate of minimum wage differs by province; therefore, the increase required in the minimum wage to put minimum wage earners above the poverty line also differs by province. The low income cut-off (LICO) was $18,421 for a single employable person in 2009 for a metropolitan area with the population over half a million

Table 7-8   Minimum Wage by Province/Territory Related to Low Income Cut-Offs

Province/Territory	Minimum General Wage *	Minimum Wage Earning 40 Hours per Week for 40 Weeks	Percent Increase Required in Minimum Wage to Arrive at LICO of $18,421
Newfoundland and Labrador	$10.00	$16,000	15
PEI	$9.30	$14,880	24
Nova Scotia	$9.65	$15,440	19
New Brunswick	$9.50	$15,200	21
Quebec	$9.65	$15,440	19
Ontario	$10.25	$16,400	12
Manitoba	$9.50	$15,200	21
Saskatchewan	$9.25	$14,800	24
Alberta	$8.80	$14,080	31
British Columbia	$8.75	$14,000	32
Yukon	$9.00	$14,400	22
Northwest Territories	$9.50	$15,200	17
Nunavut	$11.00	$17,600	4

Source: Human Resources and Skills Development Canada. n.d. "Hourly Minimum Wages in Canada for Adult Workers." *Labour*. Ottawa: Human Resources and Skills Development Canada. Last modified 2 March 2012. Available online.

(Statistics Canada 2010). The minimum wage earnings for a worker working for 40 hours for 40 weeks are given in Table 7-8 for each province. The earnings of someone working 40 hour per week, 40 weeks a year for minimum wage would have to increase by 12 percent in Ontario and by 32 percent in British Columbia to put that person above the poverty line (LICO).

Regional differences in ethnic poverty

Visible minorities, often being relatively recent migrants, tend to have higher rates of poverty. These rates vary considerably by province—from over 24 percent for Newfoundland to about 52 percent for Quebec (Table 7-9). More interestingly, there are considerable provincial variations in the differences in the poverty rate of visible minorities and that of all Canadians (Table 7-9). The lowest difference is only 23 percent, in Newfoundland, and the highest difference is 218 percent, in Nova Scotia. The visible minority population of Nova Scotia is mostly not made up of recent immigrants.

Table 7-9   Population with Low Income as a Proportion of Visible Minority and All Canadian, by Province, 1996

Province	Visible Minority (%)	All Canadian (%)	Difference between Visible Minority and All Canadian Rate (%)
Newfoundland	24.3	**19.8**	23
Prince Edward Island	28.1	11.4	**146**
Nova Scotia	**37.9**	11.9	**218**
New Brunswick	34.2	14.9	**130**
Quebec	**52.2**	**22.0**	**137**
Ontario	34.3	13.5	**154**
Manitoba	31.3	**18.8**	66
Saskatchewan	30.0	15.7	91
Alberta	31.7	14.8	**114**
British Columbia	32.0	14.6	**119**
Canada	**35.9**	**16.4**	**119**

Sources: Visible minorities: Statistics Canada. 1996. "Table 1: Visible Minorities in Canada." Statistics Profile Series. Statistics Canada Catalogue no. 85F0033MIE. Ottawa: Canadian Centre for Justice; National Council of Welfare. 1998. *Poverty Profile 1998*. Ottawa: National Council of Welfare. Available online.
Note: Numbers in bold indicate equal to or above the national average rate.

According to the 2006 census, over half of the visible minority population in Nova Scotia is black. Their ancestors fled Colonial America as slaves or freemen to settle in Nova Scotia during the 18th and 19th centuries. The high rate of poverty among visible minorities in Nova Scotia is a reflection of poverty among its black population. This shows us that not only recent immigrant characteristics, such as lack of official language proficiency, but also systemic discrimination is a factor. If recent migration characteristics were the only factors responsible for poverty among the visible minorities in Nova Scotia, then the poverty rate of visible minorities of Nova Scotia would have been much lower than that of the other provinces because the majority of the visible minorities in Nova Scotia are not recent immigrants.

Conceptual Explanation

For some regions social exclusion explains poverty, whereas for other regions the situational perspective does. Some predominantly Aboriginal peoples inhabiting remote northern areas suffer from poverty as a result of being segregated from the main economic activity areas of Canada. The poverty caused by regional remoteness can be explained by the social exclusion perspective. On the other hand, in Newfoundland, which traditionally experienced a less favourable economic situation than the rest of the country, the discovery of off-shore oil in 1997 changed it from a have-not province to a have province. Similarly, Alberta's recent economic prosperity is linked to the tar sand oil boom. This shows that the poverty situation in a region can change as the economic situation changes; in these cases, regional disparity can be explained using the situational perspective. There are certain structural situations that keep a region economically backward, and policies related to economic development can be used to bring prosperity to an economically depressed region. These policies may involve improving infrastructure such as roads, ports, airports, and communication links, and developing some viable industry. It could also include educational and training programs for the population of economically depressed regions.

Regional poverty is usually associated with exclusion of the region from the area of main economic activity and with some structural conditions that keep a specific region economically underdeveloped. The social exclusion and the situational perspectives are therefore more appropriate to explain and alleviate regional differences in poverty than are the culture of poverty and the stigma of poverty perspectives.

Chapter 8

What Goes Around Comes Around: Global Movements of Wealth

Introduction

The term *globalization* refers to the integration of the economies of nations made possible by advances in communication. The world witnessed its first steps toward globalization with the advent of improved techniques of maritime travel in the 16th century, when European powers started to colonize the Americas, Africa, and Asia. The industrialization of the 18th and 19th centuries, beginning in the United Kingdom and then spreading to other Western nations, helped to consolidate colonization and marked an unprecedented increase in the average income of populations of today's industrial nations. It also increased inequality among nations and mass poverty among today's developing nations. As wealth moved from the colonized countries of Asia, Africa, and Latin America (which we'll refer to here in shorthand as the South) to Europe and North America (here referred to as the North), the world experienced prosperity and comforts on one hand, and wars, conflicts, slavery, and human misery on the other. A second major round of globalization is now underway as a result of advances in information technology, in some cases resulting in a reverse movement of wealth. In countries such as Canada, the current information technology–based globalized economy creates either high-skill high tech jobs or low-skill services jobs. As a result, the middle class is shrinking and inequality is increasing. At the same time, the rapid economic growth of the emerging economies (such as China, India, Brazil, Russia, South Africa, Mexico, Turkey, Indonesia, Egypt, Malaysia, Thailand, Colombia, and Venezuela) is also creating increased inequality in these countries as the rich become richer and the poor become poorer. Worldwide protests related to inequality and poverty—think of Occupy Wall Street and the Arab Spring—reflect increasing tension.

This chapter explores aspects of globalization and poverty. Prior to countries of the North becoming colonizers and industrializing, many of them experienced mass poverty and underdevelopment. By contrast, countries of the South lived in relative prosperity. Colonization and industrialization reversed this disparity by transferring wealth from the South to the North. A reversal of wealth from the North to the South is underway. Since the 1980s, a rapid growth in many countries of the South and a relative economic stagnation in many countries of the North are reversing the transfer of wealth. This phenomenon is causing increased inequality across the globe. Nations have become increasingly interdependent; the poverty of one country has interrelations and repercussions for the economic prosperity of another. How will Canada's outlook be influenced by this growing trend?

The World before Colonization and Industrialization

Mass poverty is not a contemporary phenomenon. Today's developed nations experienced mass poverty during the early phases of industrialization. England began experiencing the problems of mass poverty in the 16th century, following the development of pasture farming. It was at the end of 16th century, an era of English expansion, when Queen Elizabeth toured her kingdom and returned with an observation that "paupers are everywhere" (Heilbroner 1980, 30). As wool became a profitable commodity, pastures were made by enclosing common land; this deprived peasants from self-sustenance as small "farmers." Since no factories were available at the time to offer work to these peasants, many suffered greatly, becoming an agricultural proletariat. Often peasants were forced to turn to begging, thieving, and paupery (Heilbroner 1980). Prevailing conditions in the early days of factory labour, during the inception of industrialization, were, perhaps, more horrible than what we now hear in many developing countries. As described by Heilbroner (1980), children as young as 10 years old in England were whipped day and night to stimulate the industry during the early days of industrialization. Child workers scrambled alongside pigs for the slops in a trough. They were kicked, punched, and sexually abused by their employers. There is a description of foreman pinching the child's ears until his nails passed through the flesh or a child being hung by his wrists over a machine with his knees bent and heavy weights piled over his shoulders. Working days were often up to 16 hours, with very short breaks for meals.

In England and Wales from 1601 onwards, Poor Laws were introduced, unsuccessfully, to deal with the problems of pauperism, that is, abject poverty. From the beginning of the 17th century to the end of 19th century, pauperism persisted among a progressively smaller proportion of the population. It continued well into the 20th century (Bandyopadhyaya 1988). The rest of Western Europe also went through a similar experience (Bandyopadhyaya 1988).

In the United States, millions of African slaves and American Indians paid the price of development, and many of these minorities, along with more recent Hispanic migrants, still suffer absolute poverty. In the Soviet Union, a large number of peasants paid the heavy cost of the collectivization of agriculture and forced industrialization, particularly in the 10 years between 1929 and 1939 (Bandyopadhyaya 1988). Even in Japan, where economic development seemed to have taken place smoothly in the form of state-aided capitalism, mass poverty existed not only during the Tokugawa era (1603–1868), but even after the Meiji Restoration (1868–1912) period to the early 20th century (Bandyopadhyaya 1988).

Before the colonial/industrial era, people in Africa, Asia, and the Americas lived in relative prosperity and comfort. Roche (1976) points out that Egypt was the cradle of civilization for tens of thousands of years while rest of the world lived in relative barbarism. The agricultural and the engineering systems in the Nile area were far more sophisticated than anywhere else on the globe at that time. The benefits of this development reached to South Sahara Africa, which acquired an abundance of resources. Black Africa (non-Arab) developed its social and political structures in the forms of famous ancient kingdoms of Dahomey, Benie, Songhai, and Mali (Johanson Sirleaf quoted in Roche 1976). Their social structure evolved toward the systems of morality and ethics rather than toward scientific and material pursuits (Roche 1976). At this state of civilization, Black Africa was invaded by traders and explorers from Portugal, France, Britain, and Holland. African weaponry was less deadly than European weaponry, and so Africa, against its will, began to supply labour to Europe and America. The mass poverty in many of today's developing countries is rooted in the disruption resulting from their encounter with colonizers from the West.

The impact of colonization was more dramatic on the economies of Asia in general, and on India and China in particular. In 1700, both China and India individually enjoyed a higher gross domestic product (GDP) than the total GDP of 30 Western European countries (Maddison 2008). When the British first arrived in India, in 1820, the combined share of the world GDP of China and India was 49 percent, while that of the entirety of Asia was about 60 percent. When British rule in India ended and India adopted its new constitution in 1950, its share of the world GDP had shrunk to slightly more than 4 percent. China also experienced the same fate during this period when foreign powers controlled territory in Greater China; its share also declined to less than 5 percent. Asia's share of the world GDP dropped from about 60 percent in 1820 to less than 19 percent in 1950 (Maddison 2008).

The World after Colonization and Industrialization

Three-quarters of the world's income, investment, and services, and almost all of the world's research is in the hands of one-quarter of its people—who happen to live in the northern hemisphere of the globe. And this concentration of economic power in the hands of a small group of nations is a result of international structures that developed during the colonial and post-colonial periods (Lambo 2000). The causes of the North–South gap are closely associated not only with the Industrial Revolution, but also with colonization.

The drain of capital and commodities from the colonies in the early phases of the Industrial Revolution was a major factor in the industrialization of Europe. The industrial rise of the West further aided the process of colonization, which exploited the raw materials and labour of the countries of the South. Colonial exploitation hampered the process of natural growth and blocked the economic, social, and cultural evolution of the colonized societies.

Vásquez (2001) argues that the West's escape from poverty did not occur by chance; the sustained growth over long periods of time took place in an environment that generally encouraged free enterprise and the protection of private property. Vásquez (2001) argues that today's developing countries have an advantage, because by adopting liberal economic policies, they can achieve levels of economic progress within one generation that took today's rich countries hundreds of years to achieve. High growth is possible because the poor countries will be catching up to the rich countries, rather than forging a new path; they will have the advantage of utilizing existing technologies rather than innovating new technologies. According to Vásquez (2001), studies by both the World Bank and the International Monetary Fund confirm that countries such as China and India that have chosen to liberalize their economies are indeed converging toward the industrialized world.

Vásquez (2002) cites the case of Western countries to make the point that the single most effective way to reduce world poverty is economic growth. He believes that Western countries began discovering this around 1820, when they broke with the historical norm of low growth and initiated an era of dramatic advances in material well-being. The living standards of Europe tripled and the living standards of Americans quadrupled during the 1800s (Vásquez 2002).

The recent acceleration of economic growth in many developing countries has reduced poverty, though the reduction in poverty has been uneven throughout the world. It is debatable whether market reforms that remove trade barriers and open up the economy for investment help the poor. In the past 20 years, many developing countries have liberalized their economies to varying degrees and the poor in some of these countries have seen few benefits. To illustrate impact of economic growth, Harvard economist Robert Barro (1997) notes that per capita income in the United States grew at an average of 1.75 percent per year from 1870 to 1990, making Americans the richest people in the world. We can safely conclude from the American experience that economic growth is essential for the eradication of mass poverty—in spite of its relationship with an increase in inequality.

The rapid economic growth of emerging economies such as China, India, Brazil, Indonesia, and South Africa, and globalization due to the integration of world economies is transforming global economic, political, and social systems. One of the consequences is that where high growth is increasing inequality in the developing countries, the job market is polarizing in the developed countries and inequality is increasing almost everywhere. This increase in inequality is increasing global protests and conflict.

Reversing the Trend in Wealth Transfer

A comparison of the share of the world GDP from 1950 to 2008 (Table 8-1) indicates that wealth has started to transfer from the regions of the North to those of the South. During this period, the United States' share in the world GDP declined from 27 percent to about 19 percent, and that of Western Europe from 26 percent to 17 percent. At the same time, the share of China in the world GDP has increased from less than 5 percent to more than 17 percent, and India's share in the world GDP has jumped from about 4 percent to about 7 percent.

The trend of the transfer of wealth from the South to the North has reversed. Today, Asia's share of the world GDP stands at 43.7 percent, which exceeds the combined share of 37.3 percent of North America and Western Europe (Table 8-1). China alone has a larger share of the world GDP than the 30 nations of Western Europe put together. Meanwhile, Canada's share in the world GDP has dropped, from 1.9 percent in 1950 to 1.6 percent in 2008. It may not seem much in terms of absolute figures, but this represents about a 19 percent smaller share in the world's GDP. This trend in the shift of wealth from the North to the South has immense implications for the

Table 8-1 Gross Domestic Product (GDP), 1990 International Geary-Khamis Dollars, Selected Countries and Regions, Selected Years

	1700		1820		1950		2008	
	GDP (Million)	Percent Share in World GDP	GDP (Million)	Percent Share in World GDP	GDP (Million)	Percent Share in World GDP	GDP (Million)	Percent Share in World GDP
Canada	86	0.02	738	0.1	102,164	1.9	839,199	1.6
United States	527	0.1	12,548	1.8	1,455,916	27.3	9,485,136	18.6
Total Latin America	6,346	1.7	14,921	2.2	415,328	7.8	4,045,933	7.9
Western Europe 30 Countries	80,927	21.8	158,860	22.9	1,396,287	26.2	8,698,029	17.1
China	82,800	22.3	228,600	33.0	244,985	4.6	8,908,894	17.5
India	90,750	24.5	111,417	16.1	222,222	4.2	3,415,183	6.7
Asia	229,671	61.9	412,477	59.5	990,843	18.6	22,288,543	43.7
Africa	25,692	6.9	31,161	4.5	202,646	3.8	1,734,918	3.4
World	371,058	100.0	693,502	100.0	5,335,860	100.0	50,973,935	100.0

Source: Adapted from Maddison, Angus. 2008. *Historical Statistics of World Economy 1-2008 AD*. Available online.

Note: The Geary-Khamis dollar is a hypothetical unit of currency that has the same purchasing power as the US dollar had in the United States at a given point in time.

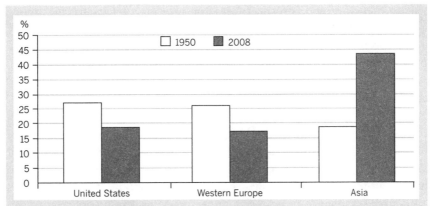

Figure 8-1   Share of World Gross Domestic Product (GDP), Selected Countries and Regions

Source: Adapted from Angus Maddison. 2008. "Table 2: GDP Levels, 1 AD–2008 AD." *Historical Statistics of the World Economy: 1–2008 AD.* Available online.

globalized world. Canada is part of this globalized world; its declining share of the world GDP could mean a declining influence in world affairs on one hand and an increasing inequality within Canadian society on the other.

Figure 8-1 shows that Asia's share in the world GDP has more than doubled from 1950 to 2008, whereas the share of the United States and the Western Europe has dropped by one-third. This trend is predicted to continue (Ward 4 January 2011).

According to a major study conducted by economists of HSBC (Ward 4 January 2011), among the top 30 economies by GDP in 2050, 19 will be countries that are presently described as emerging economies. This study further predicts that:

- world output will treble;
- the emerging economies will contribute twice as much as the developed world to global economic growth;
- the economic output of emerging economies will increase five-fold and will be larger than that of today's developed world;
- China and India, respectively, will be the largest and the third-largest economies in the world; and
- other major economies most notably will be Brazil, Russia, South Africa, Mexico, Turkey, Indonesia, Egypt, Malaysia, Thailand, Colombia, and Venezuela.

This shows that world will be quite different in the next 40 years. Another important point this study makes is that demographic patterns will influence growth prospects and the ranking of nations within the world economy. The rich countries of Europe with smaller and aging populations will be the big losers. For example, while Switzerland and the Netherlands will slip down the ranking significantly, Sweden, Belgium, Austria, Norway, and Denmark will drop out of the list of the top 30 economies altogether.

Countries such as the United States and Canada will be relatively successful at maintaining their ranking on the world GDP because they have been prudent in blunting the blow of declining fertility with the help of immigration. According to this study, the Canadian economy will maintain its present tenth rank on the share of world GDP even in 2050. This speaks louder for Canada's long-term economic and demographic policies.

Emerging economies: Catching up

The economic world is changing. Because of improvements in the determinants of economic growth, such as economic governance, human capital, and infrastructure of the emerging economies, they are developing faster than the developed economies of Canada, the United States, Europe, Australia, and Japan (Ward 4 January 2011).

Economic governance

The most significant change took place in the countries that were formerly governed by communist regimes. The Soviet Union and China were closed to trade and technological progress in the West, and as a result they suffered from low productivity and lack of technological advances (Ward 4 January 2011). These countries have opened up to trade and technology available in the West. Another big economy, India—which was fearful of British East India Company–style foreign domination—shielded its economy and domestic business from foreign competition after its independence from Britain. The result was that the Indian economy underperformed from 1947 to 1990. India removed restrictions on industrial imports and opened up its economy to Western technology in the 1990s. Latin America, along with the other emerging economies of the world, also opened up its economy to foreign competition, trade, and capital investment. These changes improved economic governance and the emerging economies put themselves on the path of high growth rates.

Human capital

An educated and healthy workforce is essential for economic output. A workforce that is well educated can acquire technological skills necessary for economic progress. Members of a healthy workforce tend to have high life expectancy which is necessary for utilizing acquired skills for a longer span of time. At the same time high life expectancy increases the old age dependency by increasing number of retired persons in the society. Therefore, increased life expectancy can be a push as well as drag for productivity. Similarly, higher fertility can be a push as well as a drag for productivity. Higher fertility increases child dependency on the workforce, but at the same time a well-educated young population provides renewal of the workforce. The quality of the workforce has improved economic output in the emerging economies, whereas the aging of the populations in the developed countries has brought down productivity.

Improvements in infrastructure

Fuelled by high economic growth, emerging economies are improving their infrastructure and are building communication systems, railways, airports, roads, and ports. Improved infrastructure is also helping the emerging economies to raise their productivity and to increase their economic growth rate.

Demographic changes

Because of declining birth rates and increasing life expectancy, population growth in the developed world will slow down. And population growth of the working age population is likely to slow down proportionately even more. According to HSBC projections, the working-age population in developed countries will continue to grow for one more decade (Ward 4 January 2011). While the workforce of Japan will shrink by 37 percent over the next 40 years, the working-age population of Saudi Arabia, which has the highest fertility rate, is expected to grow by more than 70 percent. Other parts of Asia, such as Malaysia, India, and Indonesia, will all see strong growth in their workforce. As a result of these economic and demographic changes, according to HSBC projections, the growth rate of developed economies will continue to be half that of the emerging economies over the next four decades (Ward 4 January 2011). The working-age population of Canada is projected to decline after 2030. Nevertheless, it would exceed the 2009 level even in 2061(Statistics Canada 2010).

Consequences of the Shift in Transfer of Wealth

A massive economic transformation akin to the Industrial Revolution of the early 1700s has been underway in the world since the 1980s. The improvements in communications are bringing down trade barriers between nations, enabling industries to move across international borders to save production costs. As mentioned earlier, in developed countries such as Canada and the United States, this phenomenon of globalization is eliminating labour-intensive jobs and polarizing the job market into high-skill, high-paying jobs on one hand and low-skill, low-paying jobs on the other. This has resulted in a decline in middle-income-producing manufacturing jobs, and as a consequence the middle class is shrinking. This has increased income inequality in the industrialized countries, and the less-qualified, the disadvantaged, and the discriminated-against members of society unable to find any job are destined to a life of poverty.

Increase in inequality in developed countries

As result of globalization, inequality in the world is increasing. It is manifesting in the form of protests, such as the Arab Spring and Occupy Wall Street. The Arab Spring can be explained in the light of food insecurity, unemployment, and frustrated youth (Kuhan 2011). Social inequality is cited as a root cause of the Occupy protests. So let's look at the evidence for the increase in social inequality in the selected countries of North America and Europe. In 2008, the Directorate for Employment, Labour and Social Affairs of the Organisation of Economic Co-operation and Development (OECD) published a study on its 30 member countries. The following description of inequality and poverty of four selected countries as a representative sample of the OECD countries from this report puts recent social changes in perspective in the developed world. The OECD defines poverty as the percentage of people living on less than half of the median income of the country and measures inequality in terms of earnings and net assets of the top and bottom 10 percent of the population.

The purpose of summarizing inequality and poverty levels in these selected OECD countries is to provide a perspective on the increasing inequality in recent years in the countries of North America and Europe. Economic stagnation is increasing social inequality in the developed countries, whereas rapid economic growth is increasing the gap between rich and poor in many developing countries. Historically, the increase in inequality has led to an increase in social unrest in societies.

Canada

According to the OECD (2008), for the past 10 years, rich Canadians have been getting richer, leaving both the middle and poorer income classes behind. The rich in Canada are also richer compared with their counterparts in the many other OECD countries—the average income of the richest 10 percent Canadians is US$71,000 in purchasing power parities, which is one-third above the OECD average of US$54,000 (OECD 2008). Canada's population is aging, and older people tend to have higher incomes and higher levels of accumulated assets than their younger counterparts. According to the OECD (2008), only one-fifth of the increase in income inequality in Canada is linked to changes in the age and the household structure of its population. The other four-fifths of the increase in income inequality is due to other reasons, such as polarization of job market into high-skill, high-paying jobs and low-skill, low-paying jobs.

According to the OECD (2008), inequality of household earnings has also increased significantly in Canada. Among OECD countries, only Germany saw a similar rate of increase in inequality in its household earnings during the past 10 years. Canada spends less on such cash benefits as unemployment benefits and family allowance than do most of the OECD countries. As a result, taxes and transfers do not reduce inequality in Canada by as much as they do in many other OECD countries. Between 1996 and 2005, poverty as defined by OECD (2008) has increased for all age groups in Canada, by around 2 to 3 percentage points, to an overall rate of 12 percent.

Based on OECD measures, the poverty rate of older people in Canada is 6 percent and that of children is 15 percent. Employment is more important as a way of avoiding poverty in Canada than it is in the other OECD countries. In Canadian households with no one working, two-thirds are poor. Where one person works, the poverty rate drops to 21 percent, but if there are two or more persons working in the household, the poverty rate declines to 4 percent (OECD 2008). Another feature of Canadian poverty, is that once they have fallen into poverty, Canadians are likely to remain poor for a longer span of time than do people in most OECD countries. This suggests that the increase in unemployment rates in Canada will put vulnerable groups at risk of poverty and hence will further increase inequality.

United States

After Mexico and Turkey, the United States has the highest inequality level and the highest poverty rates in the OECD. Income inequality in the United States has increased rapidly. Since 2000, rich households in the United States have been leaving both middle- and lower-income groups behind. This has happened in many countries, but nowhere has this trend been as stark as in the United States (OECD 2008). The average annual income of the richest 10 percent was US$93,000 in purchasing power parities, which was the highest among the OECD countries; however, the poorest 10 percent of Americans had an average annual income of only US$5,800, which is about 20 percent lower than the OECD average of $7,000 for this group (OECD 2008).

The distribution of earnings in the United States has widened by 20 percent since the mid-1980s, making this earnings spread the highest among the OECD countries (OECD 2008). This spread is the main reason for increasing inequality in the United States. The redistribution of income by government plays a relatively minor role in the United States compared with the other OECD countries, partly because in the United States the level of spending on social benefits such as unemployment benefits and family benefits is only 9 percent of household incomes—far below the OECD average of 22 percent (OECD 2008). The effectiveness of taxes and transfers in reducing inequality has fallen still further between 1995 to 2005 (OECD 2008). The inability of the United States to reduce inequality by redistribution of income or by raising taxes is also linked to its fiscal difficulties brought on by higher levels of debt and unemployment rates linked to global changes in economic activity.

Germany

Since 2000, income inequality and poverty have grown faster in Germany than in any other OECD country. Income inequality and poverty in Germany increased more in the five years between 2000 and 2005 than in the previous 15 years (1985–2000) combined (OECD 2008). Labour market changes have been a main driver of rising inequality in Germany. According to OECD (2008), the distribution of gross wages widened significantly after 1995, after a long period of stability. The share of jobless households has increased from 15 percent in 1995 to 19 percent in 2005, the highest among the OECD countries. More German adults and children were living in poverty in 2005 than in 1995. This indicates that inequality in Germany has increased over these 10 years.

Italy

According to the OECD study (2008), during the early 1990s, income inequality and poverty grew rapidly in Italy. Italy now has the sixth-largest gap between rich and poor of all 30 OECD countries. Incomes from work, capital, and savings have become 33 percent more unequal since the mid-1980s (OECD 2008). This is the highest increase in inequality among the OECD countries. And it took place despite the fact that Italy has partly offset the growing gap between rich and poor by increasing household taxation and spending more on social benefits for poor people. This is unusual among OECD countries (OECD 2008).

The average income of the poorest 10 percent Italians is around US$5,000 in purchasing power parities, which is below the OECD average of $7,000; the average income of the richest 10 percent Italians is $55,000, which is above the OECD average. The rich have benefited more from the economic growth than have the poor or the middle classes (OECD 2008).

Inequality and economic growth in developing countries

Projections made by HSBC (Ward 4 January 2011) suggest that 19 emerging economies, which include the so-called BRICS (Brazil, Russia, India, China, and South Africa), will dominate the world economic scene over the next 40 years and that economic dominance will shift from Europe and North America to the southern hemisphere. The rapid economic growth in many of these countries is also causing increased inequality. As a sample of emerging economies, let us look at inequality situation in the two largest emerging economies—China and India. There is some evidence from these both countries that inequality increases during the period of economic growth, which is a cause of fear of social unrest.

China

Income distribution is crucial in an economy that has a high growth rate because high growth also has the potential of concentrating income in the hands of a particular group, occupation, or geographical area. In China, manufacturing has contributed to rapid economic growth. Because manufacturing is usually concentrated in urban areas, it increases inequality between rural and urban areas, as well as within urban areas. The available evidence suggests that in China inequality has increased not only between rural and urban areas but also the overall inequality has increased. The Gini coefficient is a measure of inequality of distribution of income—a value of 0 means total equality and a value of 1 means maximum inequality. China's national level Gini coefficient has increased from 0.30 in 1978 to 0.45 in 2002, an increase of 50 percent (United Nations Development Programme [UNDP] 2005). Over 40 percent of this growth in inequality is due to rural–urban inequality—the Gini coefficient for rural areas increased from 0.21 to 0.38 and that for the urban area from 0.16 to 0.34 during the post-reform period of 1978–2002 (UNDP 2005). This means that during the high-growth post-reform era, inequality in China increased by 80 percent in rural areas and by 113 percent in urban areas.

India

According to Ghosh (2010) the adjusted data shows that the rural inequality went up in India between 1993–1994 and 1999–2000. Regional differences are also significant and have increased recently; the ratio of the per capita gross domestic product of the richest major state (Punjab) to that of the poorest major state (Bihar) increased from 2.2 in 1980 to 4.8 in 2004

(Pal and Ghosh 2007). That means that inequality between the richest and the poorest states has increased from two times to almost five times during the post-1990s economic growth period. We can say that the state of Punjab, which was two times richer than the state of Bihar in 1980, had become five times richer over the high economic growth period. According to the OECD (2011), earnings inequality has significantly increased in India since the 1990s; the ratio between earnings of the top and bottom 10 percent of the population has doubled from six times to 12 times.

Conflicts and Conflagrations

While economic stagnation is increasing social inequality in the developed countries, rapid economic growth is increasing the gap between the rich and the poor in many developing countries. An increase in social inequality is endemic to almost all the emerging economies (OECD 2011). Inequality is perceived as injustice. The perception of injustice breeds discontent and, hence, protests and conflicts in societies. Today's Arab Spring and Occupy Wall Street protests are rooted in the fear of increasing inequality in the world. Social inequality that is perceived as widespread deprivation has historically been a major driver of many revolutions. The storming of Bastille in 1789 was the result of humiliation felt by the protesters after Queen Marie Antoinette's words "let them eat cake."

The Arab Spring protests and inequality

The beginning of the Arab Spring protests is as poignant as that of the storming of the Bastille. Mohammed Boueizi, a young man of 25, was surviving by selling fruit in a small town in Tunisia. He refused to pay a bribe to a policeman, who then destroyed his cart. No longer able to earn a livelihood to support his family, the humiliated Mohammed immolated himself on 17 December 2010. He died from his burns on 4 January 2011. Within these 17 days, word of his action spread throughout Tunisia through Internet social media, and demonstrations started across the country demanding equality and justice. This was the beginning of the Arab Spring movement.

Civil servants in the US state of Wisconsin who protested in late February 2011 against cuts in their payments shouted slogans like "We are all Egyptians" and the Chinese censorship blocks the notion of "Jasmine," trying to avert any potential spill-over of the virus of the Jasmine revolution that started in Tunisia on 17 December 2010 (Kneissl 2011). The Tunisian revolution spread to other Arab countries and the term *Arab Spring*, referring to mass protests against dictatorship, social inequality, and injustice, became popular in the media.

The Occupy protests and inequality

The Occupy Wall Street movement drew attention to increasing inequality in the United States. The protesters often referred to the notion that the economy has generated unequal outcomes, whereby the top 1 percent have benefitted enormously, leaving behind the remaining 99 percent. To some extent it is true that the growth in income of the top 1 percent of the population that has the highest incomes in the United States has been much larger than the growth in income for the rest of the population. A US budget paper (Congressional Budget Office [CBO] 2011) summarized that for the top 1 percent of the population with the highest income, the average after-tax household income grew by 275 percent between 1979 and 2007, whereas for the 20 percent of the population with the lowest income, average after-tax household income grew by only 18 percent over this same period. As a result of this uneven income growth, the distribution of after-tax household income in the United States was substantially more unequal in 2007 than in 1979 (CBO 2011).

The resentment about this polarization of economic rewards and social inequality has been further exacerbated by high unemployment among recent college graduates, deteriorating wages, disappearing pension plans, home foreclosings, and increasing poverty (Brown 2011).

The high economic growth in the emerging economies is increasing social inequality, and that, in turn, is fuelling social unrest in these countries. In China, demonstrations for which Chinese authorities use a term *mass incidence* were unknown before Tiananmen Square demonstrations in 1989 but have become quite common in recent decades. The number of demonstrations has doubled from 87,000 in 2005 to 180,000 in 2010 (Sun 2011). Lum (2006) believes that growing disparities in income, official corruption, and a lack of democratic institutions are likely to continue to fuel social unrest in China. The situation is not very different in democratic India, the second-fastest growing large economy in the world. Because democracy in India makes harder for government to clamp down, demonstrations can start spontaneously. India tried to create geographical regions with more free-market oriented laws on a pattern similar to Special Economic Zones (SEZs) in China. Recently, there have been massive demonstrations in India against the so-called SEZs, rising inflation fuelled by rapid growth, and corruption.

Canada's Position in the Changing World

Increasing social inequality and economic uncertainty is instilling a fear of social unrest in the developed as well as the developing countries. Canada seems to be better insulated from social and economic turmoil at this time. Let us look at the prognosis for Canada's future.

Canada has endured the 2008 financial crisis and economic slowdown much better than the United States and Europe. The Occupy Toronto and the Occupy Vancouver protests were a milder form of Occupy Wall Street. According to the 2008 OECD study, although poverty rates are high in Canada in relative terms, absolute poverty is low. This study further shows that compared with other OECD countries, in Canada, fewer households struggle to purchase basic goods and to have decent housing and living conditions, and social mobility is higher. This study also points out that the children of poor parents in Canada stand a reasonably good chance of becoming non-poor, and vice versa. It is not surprising, then, that Canada's Gini coefficient, at 0.326, is 25 percent lower than that of the United States (UNDP 2011).

One of the fears is that as the population ages in the developed countries, health care expenditures may further stretch national budgets and may also increase social inequality. Canada spends only 9.8 percent of its GDP on its universally accessible health care, compared with the 15.2 percent that the United States spends on its current inequitable system (World Health Organization 2011).

Projections of Canada's economic indicators by HSBC (Ward 4 January 2011) for the next 40 years are much more favourable. The study indicates that though several countries of the North will lose their ranking to emerging economies, Canada's rank on share of world GDP will remain unchanged at 10th position even in 2050 because Canada's GDP is expected to grow at a healthy average annual rate of about 2.3 percent for the next 40 years (Ward 4 January 2011).

The HSBC study also paints a fairly stable demographic picture for Canada. Canada's working population will grow at an annual rate of 0.4 percent in the decade 2020–2030 and 0.3 percent in the decade of 2040–2050. As a result, the working-age population of Canada will increase by almost 12 percent in the next 40 years, whereas it will decline in most of the European countries. Though Canada's fertility will remain below the replacement level, it will be compensated for by immigration. Unlike the European countries and Japan, Canada is likely to continue to refresh its workforce though immigration.

Canada's main trading partner, the United States, though it is expected to lose its rank in the share of the world GDP to China, will still be the second-largest economy in the world in 2050 (Ward 4 January 2011). Canada has already started diversifying its trade with the emerging economies. Therefore, Canada's diversified trade and its proximity to the second-largest economy of the world will keep its balance of trade healthy even in

2050. Though the emerging economies will grow faster, their populations will also grow larger, and that will result in many talented persons from these countries seeking immigration to Canada. After all, Europeans continued to migrating to Canada even during the post–World War II prosperity in Europe. With this economic and demographic scenario, Canada is likely to remain a leading economy and a beacon of peace and tranquility over the next 40 years.

Defining and Measuring Poverty in Canada

Introduction

According to Whyte (1965), one of the earliest and most explicit formulations of poverty defined in terms of subsistence is found in Malthus's first essay on population. Malthus (1826) postulated that

1. sexual passion remains at a constant level;
2. population grows at a geometric progression (2, 4, 8, 16 ...) and resources (food) grow at an arithmetic progression (1, 2, 3, 4 ...); and
3. therefore, population, if not controlled by abstinence, will be controlled by such natural checks as famine, disease, and war.

Malthus claimed that this would cause an imbalance between population growth and the food supply. As a result of this imbalance, a segment of the society would be undernourished and poor. Malthus foresaw increasing poverty because he believed that human sexual passion and the need for food are unlikely to diminish.

Another early formulation is social Darwinism, derived from Darwin's theory of natural selection and survival of the fittest (1859). According to Darwin, all species overproduce. This results in a struggle for survival among species. The fittest members of the species are selected by nature to propagate their species. Though the term *social Darwinism* existed in Europe since 1877, Spencer (1961) coined the phrase *survival of the fittest* and applied Darwin's principles of natural selection to human society. According to Spencer's concept of social Darwinism, just as there is a struggle for survival among species, there are conflicts between social groups, and it is the best-adapted groups who survive these conflicts. Social Darwinism is an elitist belief stating that the strongest or fittest should survive and flourish in society, while the weak and unfit should be allowed to die. Those who adhere to Spencer's idea of social Darwinism consider poverty as "unfitness." Cooley (1925), a founding father of American sociology, argued that poverty is unfitness in a social sense, not in a biological sense. Cooley considered poverty an "unintended consequence" of economic development and concluded that the main cause of poverty is maladjustment between individual or family or neighbourhood group and the wider society (Whyte 1965).

In the early 20th century, as industrialization brought affluence, a large section of the population was freed from the subsistence level of poverty. Growing confidence in science and technology precluded the possibility of poverty ever again becoming a serious social problem in industrialized countries. While the economic depression of the 1930s marred this optimism, it did confirm Cooley's conclusion that causes of poverty are economic in nature. As a result, efforts to define poverty in terms of economics followed.

Defining Poverty

The terms frequently used in the sociological literature are *objective poverty* and *subjective poverty*. Individuals who are unable to fulfil their minimal needs of subsistence in terms of food, clothing, and shelter manifest objective poverty. Subjective poverty is also called relative deprivation. According to this concept, individuals or families compare themselves with an "average individual" or an "average family." If their resources fall seriously short of this "average individual" or "average family," they feel deprived even though they may have enough to feed and clothe themselves.

In developed countries such as Canada, a considerable level of poverty is experienced in terms of relative deprivation. Although some of the poor in Canada are unable to fulfil minimal absolute needs of subsistence in terms of food, clothing or shelter, the majority suffer from subjective poverty. The resources of these poor people fall seriously short of those of the average individual or the average family. Statistics Canada and other agencies use various methods to calculate this average. This average that separates the poor from the non-poor is termed *a poverty line*.

Poverty lines are based on the average household income, on the amount spent on a basket of basic necessities, or on the proportion of income spent on basic necessities such as food, clothing, and shelter. Some poverty lines may be income-based while the others may be expenditure-based; they all use an average (a line) to separate the poor from the non-poor.

Measuring Poverty in Canada

Canada has no official definition of poverty. Different organizations in Canada measure poverty in different ways. However, most prevailing measures of poverty in Canada use as their benchmark some form of poverty line.

Statistics Canada's low income cut-offs (LICOs)

Statistics Canada is the premier statistical agency of Canada. Its low income cut-offs (LICOs) have been informally used by researchers to measure poverty in Canada since the late 1960s. Statistics Canada (1999) emphasizes that the LICOs only reflect a methodology that identifies populations who are substantially worse off than the average. The LICOs are not intended to serve as official poverty lines of the federal government, but in the absence of an accepted definition of poverty, these statistics have been used by many analysts who wanted to study the characteristics of the relatively worse off individuals and families in Canada.

LICOs were originally developed from family expenditure data derived from the census. At present, Statistics Canada collects data on consumer expenditure by survey. The information from the consumer finance survey is used to calculate the *average* amount a Canadian household spends on basic necessities—that is, food, shelter, and clothing. The low income cut-off is set where households spend 20 percent more than the amount spent by an average Canadian household on these basic items. Any individual or family with an income lower than this level can be considered to be living in hardship.

When these cut-offs were first established in 1961, the average proportion of income spent on food, clothing, and shelter was 50 percent. Therefore, households that spent 70 percent or more of their income on these basic necessities were considered to be living with financial hardship. Because annual family expenditure data was not available, the measure was adjusted annually according to the cost of living, the consumer price index. Whenever new family expenditure data became available, these low income cut-offs were evaluated, leading to revisions in 1969, 1978, 1986, and 1992. In 1978, the average Canadian household spent 38.8 percent of its income on such basic necessities as food, shelter, and clothing. Thus in 1978, LICOs were set where households spent 58.8 percent or more of their income on basic necessities. According to Statistics Canada's 1992 Family Expenditure Survey, the average Canadian household spent 34.7 percent of its income on necessities. Households that spent more than 54.7 percent of income on food, shelter and clothing were thus considered to be living below the low income cut-off (Statistics Canada 1998).

The low income cut-offs are calculated for seven family sizes and five population sizes of the place of residence to form a set of 35 cut-offs. Table A1-1 illustrates these 35 low income cut-offs for 2009.

The main criticism of the low income cut-offs methodology is that the 20 percent factor is arbitrarily selected, and that the cut-offs are not revised annually.

Table A1-1   Statistics Canada's Low Income Cut-Offs (1992-based) in Current Dollars, by Population of Area of Residence and Family Size, 2009

Family Size	Rural Areas	Less than 30,000*	30,000 to 99,000	100,000 to 499,999	500,000 and over
	Area of Residence Size				
	After Taxes				
1 person	12,050	13,791	15,384	15,579	18,421
2 persons	14,666	16,785	18,725	18,960	22,420
3 persons	18,263	20,900	23,316	23,610	27,918
4 persons	22,783	26,075	29,089	29,455	34,829
5 persons	25,944	29,692	33,124	33,541	39,660
6 persons	28,773	32,929	36,736	37,198	43,984
7 or more persons	31,602	36,167	40,346	40,854	48,308
	Before Taxes				
1 person	15,302	17,409	19,026	19,144	22,229
2 persons	19,050	21,672	23,685	23,832	27,674
3 persons	23,419	26,643	29,118	29,299	34,022
4 persons	28,435	32,349	35,354	35,573	41,307
5 persons	32,250	36,690	40,097	40,345	46,850
6 persons	36,374	41,380	45,223	45,504	52,838
7 or more persons	40,496	46,071	50,350	50,661	58,827

Source: Statistics Canada, Income Statistics Division. 2010. *Low Income Lines 2008–09.* Statistics Canada Catalogue no. 75F002M -No. 005. Ottawa: Statistics Canada. Available online.
*Includes cities with a population between 15,000 and 30,000 and small urban areas (population under 15,000).

Statistics Canada's low income measure (LIM)

Since 1988, Statistics Canada has been reviewing the low income cut-offs. A discussion paper examining a wide range of alternative measures of low incomes concluded that there is no one measure superior to the others and that no measure is free of subjectivity (Wolfson and Evans 1989). According to Statistics Canada (2010), the low income measure (LIM) is the most commonly used low-income line for making international comparisons. The LIM is fixed at 50 percent of the median income, adjusted for the household size. A household is composed of a person or a group of persons residing in a dwelling. The household size is adjusted to the means (income) a household requires. The assumption is that the larger the size of the household, the greater are its needs. For example, a household with four persons needs a higher income than a household with only two persons to have the equivalent standard of living. There is no agreement on the amount of extra income required by a larger household to have a standard of living equivalent to the smaller household. This lack of agreement introduces subjectivity to LIMs. Nevertheless, the review found that the LIM is a potentially viable alternative to the low income cut-offs and has the advantage of being a self-updating measure because it does not require either family expenditure data or consumer price index data for updating because it is calculated annually using an annual survey of household income. Unlike the low income cut-offs, which are derived from an expenditure survey and then compared with an income survey, the LIMs are both derived and applied using a single income survey.

Before the changes were introduced in 2010, Statistics Canada (1998) used family income instead of household income and assumed that in comparison to the need of the first adult, the need for each additional adult increases by 40 percent and for each child by 30 percent. These values were called "equivalent of scales." Based on these simple assumptions, the LIMs were calculated taking the following four steps:

1. Determine the adjusted family size by counting the first adult as one person and each additional adult as 0.4 of a person, and each child under 16 years of age as 0.3 of a person (except in a family of one adult and one child only, where the first child is counted as 0.4 of a person).
2. For each family, divide its income by adjusted family size to obtain adjusted family income.
3. Determine the median income adjusted by family size, which is the value where 50 percent of families have a lower adjusted income and 50 percent have a higher adjusted income.
4. Use 50 percent of this median adjusted family income as the LIM.

As mentioned earlier, a lack of agreement on the extra income required by a larger family to have a standard of living equivalent to that of a smaller family introduced subjectivity to the LIMs. In 2010, Statistics Canada made some revisions to ensure international consistency. In this revision, Statistics Canada first calculates "equivalent household income" for each household as follows:

1. Divide household income by its adjusted size. (The adjusted household size is the square root of the number of persons in the household.)

Table A1-2   Low Income Measures (LIMs) by Income and Household Size, 2008

Household Size	Market Income	Before Tax	After Tax
1	18,822	21,189	18,582
2	26,618	29,966	26,279
3	32,601	36,700	32,185
4	37,644	42,378	37,164
5	42,087	47,380	41,551

Source: Statistics Canada, Income Statistics Division. 2010. *Low Income Lines 2008–09*. Statistics Canada Catalogue no. 75F002M – No. 005. Ottawa: Statistics Canada. Available online.

2. Assign this adjusted household income to each individual in the population.
3. Determine the median of this "equivalent household income" over the population of individuals. (The median is where half of all individuals will be above this income and half will be below.)
4. For the LIM for a household of one person, use 50 percent of this "equivalent household income."
5. For the LIMs for other household sizes, multiply this LIM value for a one-person household by these households' "equivalent household size."

Three types of LIMs are calculated: market income, before-tax income, and after-tax income using Statistics Canada's Survey of Labour and Income Dynamics (SLID). For example, the LIM based for a one-person household under market income in Table A1-2 is $18,822; the LIM for a two-person household size is $18,822 X $\sqrt{2}$ = $26,618; and that of four-person household is $18,822 X $\sqrt{4}$ = $37,644.

Canadian Council on Social Development poverty lines

While Statistics Canada's low income cut-offs (LICOs) are based on the idea of proportion of income spent on the basic necessities, the Canadian Council on Social Development uses the concept of income inequality. According to this approach, those households living on 50 percent of the Canadian average family income are living under the poverty line. This method also involves centring the poverty line by applying the average family income for Canada to a particular household unit. For example, if in 2008 the average family size in Canada was 3.0 persons and the average family income for a family of three was $85,000, the poverty line for a family of three persons in that year would be $42,500, half of the average family income for this size of family.

The council applies a weighting system to adjust the poverty lines for households of different sizes. A family of one person gets three income units, a family of two persons gets five units, a family of three gets six units, and each larger sized family gets one additional unit.

The poverty line for a family of two persons that gets five units can be calculated by dividing the poverty line for a three-person family by its units; that is, 6 units and then multiplying by the number of units of a two-person family. As mentioned earlier, the poverty line for a family of three person was $42,500 in 2008; therefore, the poverty line for a family of two persons in 2008 was ($42,500/6) × 5 = $35,416.

The Special Senate Committee on Poverty: Poverty lines

The Special Senate Committee on Poverty (1971) arrived at a set of poverty lines based on expenditure rather than income. The senate committee assigned family size equalizer points (FSEPs) to adjust for family size. A family of one received three points, a family of two received five points, a family of three received six points, and so on. The committee's poverty lines change in terms of changing values of the equalizer points. In the base year of 1969, the total disposable income in Canada was $43 billion. Based on the number of families in Canada with different family sizes, the total number of FSEPs was estimated at 38 million. When $43 billion is divided by 38 million, the result is $1,126. This figure represented the average per-capita living standard for the base year of 1969. This amount of $1,126 is used to adjust the average standards of living for any year for which poverty lines are to be calculated.

According to the Social Planning Council of Metropolitan Toronto (1983), the ratio of total disposable income and the total number of FSEPs in 1983 resulted in the value of the average living standard being $2,038. Using this value, the poverty line for a family of two for 1983 could be calculated as follows:

1. FSEPs assigned to a family of two = 5
2. Guaranteed annual income for the family of two =
   $2,038 × 5 = $10,190
3. The senate committee assumed that this estimated guaranteed annual income is only 70 percent of the poverty line. Therefore, the poverty line for the family of two would be its guaranteed annual income divided by 70 percent: $10,190 divided by 0.7 = $14,557.

Table A1-3   Poverty Lines Based on the Special Senate Committee on Poverty Formula, by Family Size, 1983 and 2010

Family Size	Family Size Equalizer Points	Value of One Family Size Equalizer Point	Guaranteed Income 1983[a]	Poverty Line 1983[b]	Poverty Line 2010[c]
1	3	$2,038	$6,114	$8,734	$17,373
2	5	$2,038	$10,190	$14,557	$28,954
3	6	$2,038	$12,228	$17,469	$34,744
4	7	$2,038	$14,266	$20,380	$40,536
5	8	$2,038	$16,034	$23,292	$45,559

Sources: Adapted from The Special Senate Committee on Poverty. 1971. *Poverty in Canada*. Ottawa: Information Canada, 213–216; Social Planning Council of Metropolitan Toronto. 1983. *Social Infopac*. Toronto: Social Planning Council of Metropolitan Toronto, 5.
[a]Obtained by multiplying the number of family size equalizer points by $2,038
[b]Derived by considering the guaranteed income as 70 percent of poverty, 100/70; Poverty line for Family Size 1 $6,114/0.7 = $8,734
[c]Derived by applying change in the consumer price index to 1983 poverty lines.

Using this logic, the Social Planning Council of Metropolitan Toronto calculated the poverty line for 1983 (Table A1-3). These 1983 poverty lines are adjusted to the cost of living (the consumer price index) to arrive at the poverty lines for 2010.

Market basket measure (MBM)

The market basket measure is based on the cost of a minimum basket of goods and services that would support a basic standard of living in a community. This minimum basket of goods and services includes the costs of food, clothing, footwear, transportation, shelter, and expenses for other basic necessities. In 2010, Statistics Canada (2010) calculated MBM thresholds using a nutritious diet as specified in the 2008 National Nutritious Food Basket. This minimum basket includes costs of food, clothing, footwear, transportation, shelter, and other expenses required for a basic standard of living by a reference family of two adults aged 25 to 49 years and two children aged 9 and 13 years. The shelter cost includes the median cost of electricity, heat, water, and appliances of a two- or three-bedroom unit; transportation costs included public transit costs where available or costs associated with owning and operating a modest vehicle where public transit is not available. This cost is calculated for the reference family of

Table A1-4   Market Basket Measure (MBM) Thresholds, Disposable Income by Family Size and Regions, Ontario, 2008

Household Size	Rural	Less than 30,000	30,000 to 99,999	100,000 to 499,999	Ottawa	Hamilton/ Burlington	Toronto
1	13,878	14,452	13,310	14,022	14,899	13,954	15,565
2	19,626	20,438	18,823	19,830	21,070	19,733	22,012
3	24,037	25,032	23,054	24,287	25,805	24,168	26,959
4	27,756	28,904	26,620	28,044	29,797	27,907	31,129
5	31,032	32,316	29,762	31,354	33,314	31,201	34,803

Source: Statistics Canada, Income Statistics Division. 2010. *Low Income Lines 2008–09*. Statistics Canada Catalogue no. 75F002M -No. 005. Ottawa: Statistics Canada. Available online.

two adults and two children. To calculate the MBM threshold for the other family sizes, the value of the MBM threshold of the reference family of four is divided by the square root of its size and then multiplied by the square root of the desired family size. For example, to calculate an MBM for the household size of five in a rural area of Ontario, the MBM of $27,756 from Table A1-4 is divided by the square root of 4 and then multiplied by the square root of 5: ($27,756/$\sqrt{4}$) × ($\sqrt{5}$) = $31,032.

Weaknesses of poverty measures

All poverty measures have their strengths and weaknesses. Statistics Canada's low income cut-offs, low income measures, and basic market basket are based on the household size and the population of the place of residence, and are calculated from the national survey, but they do not take into account the variations in local markets.

In addition, the concept of goods and services deemed necessary for a proper social and physical development, though based on a national survey, has the disadvantage of an arbitrary benchmark selected at 50 percent of the average family income.

The adequacy of income support programs

One of the advantages of these measures of poverty line, however, is that they are useful in assessing the adequacy of social assistance and income maintenance programs. There are a large number of income support programs in Canada, which are administered by the three levels of government (federal, provincial, and municipal). Welfare incomes from basic social assistance, family allowance payments, child tax credit, child-related benefits, federal sales tax rebates, and provincial tax credits can be compared against different types of poverty lines to assess the adequacy of these programs.

Statistics Canada's low income cut-offs (LICOs) have the advantage of being available for a longer historical period. The LICOs are also used by the National Council of Welfare, which besides Statistics Canada, is our another major source of data. Therefore, in this book, LICOs are used as measures of poverty unless otherwise noted.

References

Adam, Ian, William Cameron, Brian Hill, and Peter Penz. 1971. *The Real Poverty Report.* Edmonton: M. G. Hertig Ltd.

Albanese, Patrizia. 2010. *Child Poverty in Canada.* Don Mills: Oxford University Press.

Alcock, P. 1993. *Understanding Poverty.* Basingstoke, UK: Macmillan.

Armitage, Andrew. 1988. *Social Welfare in Canada.* Toronto: McClelland and Stewart.

Armstrong, P., and H. Armstrong. 1978. *The Double Ghetto: Canadian Women and Their Segregated Work.* Toronto: McClelland and Stewart.

———. 1987. "Looking Ahead: The Future of Women's Work in Australia and Canada." In *Feminism and Political Economy* edited by H. J. Maroney and M. Luxton, 312–32. Toronto: Methuen.

Balakrishnan, T.R., John Kantner, and J.D. Allingham. 1975. *Fertility and Family Planning in a Canadian Metropolis.* Montreal: McGill-Queen's University Press.

Bandyopadhyaya, Jayantanuja. 1988. *The Poverty of Nations.* New Delhi: Allied Publishers.

Banfield, Edward C. 1970. *The Unheavenly City.* Boston: Little, Brown.

Bank of Canada. 2011. Available online.

Barro, Robert J. 1997. *Determinants of Economic Growth: A Cross-Country Empirical Study.* Cambridge, MA: MIT Press.

Basavarajappa, K.G., and Ravi B.P. Verma. 1985. "Asian Immigrants in Canada: Some Findings from 1981 Census." *International Migration* 23: 97–121.

Battle, Ken. 2003. *Minimum Wages in Canada: A Statistical Portrait with Policy Implications.* Ottawa: Caledon Institute of Social Policy.

Beaujot, R., K.G. Basavarajappa, and R.B.P. Verma. 1988. *Income of Immigrants in Canada.* Statistics Canada Catalogue no. 91-527-E Occasional. Ottawa: Statistics Canada. Available online.

Beaujot, Roderic, and Jianye Liu. 2004. "Social assistance, custody and child poverty: cross-national comparison." Paper presented at poster session 3-4 of Population Association of America. Boston, April.

Bergmann, Barbara R. 1987. "Women's Role in Economy: Teaching the Issue." *The Journal of Economic Education* 18 (4).

Black, Debra. 1989a. "No Place to Grow." *The Toronto Star*, 23 January. B1.

———. 1989b. "A Tough Time in Childhood." *The Toronto Star*, 28 January. H1.

Black, Errol, and Lisa Shaw. 1998. *The Case for a Strong Minimum Wage Policy.* Winnipeg: The Canadian Centre for Policy Alternatives.

Brewis, T.N. 1970. "Problems of Regional Disparities." In *Poverty and Social Policy in Canada*, edited by W. E. Mann, 208–26. Toronto: The Copp Clark Publishing Company.

Brown, Wendy. 2011. "Occupy Wall Street: Return of a Repressed Res-Publica." *Theory and Events* 14 (4). Available online.

Buckland, Lin. 1985. "Education and Training: Equal Opportunities or Barrier to Employment?" In *Research Studies of the Commission on Equality in Employment* (April): 131–156. Ottawa: Ministry of Supply and Services.

Campaign2000. 2005. "Decision Time for Canada: Let's Make Poverty History 2005." *Report Card on Child Poverty in Canada.* Toronto: Campain2000. Available online.

Canada. Aboriginal Affairs and Northern Development Canada. 2012. *Self-Government.* Gatineau, Quebec. Available online.

———. Beaudoin-Dobbie Committee. 1992. *A Report of Parliament's Special Joint Committee on a Renewed Canada.* Ottawa: Government of Canada.

————. Commission for the Review of Social Assistance in Ontario. 2011. *A Discussion Paper: Issues and Ideas.* Toronto: Queen's Printer. Available online.

————. Department of Indian and Northern Affairs (DIAND). 1980. *Indian Conditions: A Survey.* Ottawa: Department of Indian and Northern Affairs.

————. Economic Council of Canada. 1976. *People and Jobs.* Ottawa: Information Canada.

————. Economic Council of Canada. 1977. *Living Together: A Study in Disparities.* Ottawa: Ministry of Supply and Services Canada.

————. Economic Council of Canada. 1990. *Good Jobs, Bad Jobs.* Ottawa: Economic Council of Canada.

————. Government of Canada. 24 November 1989. *Hansard.* Ottawa: Queen's Printer.

————. Health and Welfare Canada, Policy Research and Strategic Planning Branch. 1979. *The Incomes of Elderly Canadians in 1975.* Ottawa: Health and Welfare Canada.

————. Health Canada. 2002a. *A Statistical Profile on the Health of First Nations in Canada.* Ottawa: Government of Canada.

————. Health Canada. 2002b. *Healthy Canadians—A Federal Report on Comparable Health Indicators 2002.* Ottawa: Health Canada.

————. Human Resources and Social Development Canada (HRSDC). 2005. *The Changing Face of Canadian Workplaces—Why Work-Life Balance Is an Issue.* Ottawa: Human Resources and Social Development Canada. Available online.

————. Human Resources Development. 2001. "Recent Immigrants Have Experienced Unusual Economic Difficulties." *Applied Research Bulletin* Winter/Spring 7 (1).

————. Human Resources Development. 2002. *Knowledge Matters: Canada's Innovation Strategy.* Ottawa: Government of Canada. Available online.

————. Indian Affairs and Northern Development, First Nations and Northern Statistics Section. 2001. *Basic Departmental Data, 2001.* Ottawa: Government of Canada.

————. Indian and Northern Affairs. 2002. *Highlights of the Third Survey of First Nations People Living On-reserve.* Ottawa: Government of Canada. Available online.

————. Indian and Northern Affairs (INAC). 2011. *Self Government.* Ottawa: Government of Canada. Available online.

————. Interprovincial Task Force. 1980. *The Income Security in Canada.* Ottawa: Canadian Intergovernmental Conference Secretariat.

————. Law Reform Commission of Canada. 1976. *Family Law: Enforcement of Maintenance Orders.* Ottawa: Information Canada.

————. Royal Commission on the Status of Women (The Abella Report). 1984. *Report of the Royal Commission on the Status of Women.* Ottawa: Information Canada.

————. Royal Commission on the Status of Women. 1970. *Report of the Royal Commission on the Status of Women.* Ottawa: Information Canada.

————. Special Senate Committee on Poverty. 1971. *Poverty in Canada—The Report on the Special Senate Committee on Poverty.* Ottawa: Information Canada.

Canadian Council in Learning. 2007. "Gender Differences in Career Choices: Why Girls Don't Like Science." *Lessons in Learning.* Ottawa: Canadian Council in Learning. Available online.

Canadian Council of Social Development (CCSD). Quoted in Campaign2000. 2005. "Decision Time for Canada: Let's Make Poverty History 2005." *Report Card on Child Poverty in Canada.* Toronto: Campain2000. Available online.

————. 2000. *The Canadian Fact Book on Poverty.* Ottawa: Canadian Council on Social Development.

Canadian Institute of Child Health. 2000. *The Health of Canada's Children.* 3rd ed. Ottawa: Canadian Institute of Child Health.

Canadian Women's Foundation (CWF). 2011. "Moving Women Out of Poverty." Fact Sheet. Toronto: CWF. Available online.

Chen, Wen-Hao. 2005. *Examining the Working Poor in Canada: Is Working a Ticket Out of Poverty?* Ottawa: Statistics Canada (Family and Labour Studies). Available online.

Clausen, John A., and Melvin Kohn. 1959. "Relationship of Schizophrenia to the Social Structure of a Small City." In *Epidemiology of Mental Disorder*, edited by Benjamin Pasamanick, 69–86. Washington, DC: American Association for the Advancement of Science.

Clodman, J., and A.H. Richmond. 1981. *Immigration and Unemployment.* Toronto: Institute for Behavioural Research, York University.

Coates, Mary Lou. 1988. *Part-Time Employment: Labour Market Flexibility and Equity Issues.* Kingston: Industrial Relations Centre, Queen's University.

Cooley, Charles H. 1925. *Social Organization.* New York: Schocken Books.

CTV. 2004. "Toronto Ghettos Shifting to the Suburbs: Report." CTVNews, 5 April. Available online.

Darwin, Charles. 1859. *Origin of Species.* London: John Murray.

Davis, Allison. 1948. *Social Class Influences Upon Learning.* Cambridge, MA: Harvard University Press.

Dougherty, G.E. *Socioeconomic Differences in Paediatric Mortality in Urban Canada: 1981.* 1986. Master's Thesis. Montreal: McGill University, Department of Epidemiology and Biostatistics. Quoted in Shah et al. 1987. "The Health of Children of Low-Income Families." *Canadian Medical Association Journal* 137(September 15): 485–490.

Duncan, Greg, and Jeanne Brooks-Gunn. Quoted in JRank. 2008. *Consequences of Poverty, Children Poor Families Effects.* Available online.

Dunham, H. Warren. 1965. *Community and Schizophrenia: An Epidemiological Analysis.* Detroit: Wayne State University Press.

Dunphy, Catherine. 1989. "Only a Dream." *The Toronto Star*, 27 January. B1–B4.

Ever, S.E., and C.G. Rand. 1983. "Morbidity in Canadian Indian and Non-Indian Children in the Second Year." *Canadian Journal of Public Health* 74: 191–194.

Ferrao, Vincent. 1 April 2011. "Paid Work." *Women in Canada: A Gender-Based Statistical Report.* Statistics Canada Catalogue no. 89-503-X. Ottawa: Statistics Canada. Available online.

Fleury, Dominique, and Myriam Fortin. 2006. *When Working Is Not Enough to Escape Poverty: An Analysis of Canada's Poor.* Ottawa: Human Resources and Social Development Canada. Available online.

———, M. Fortin. and M. Luong. 2005. "What Does It Mean to be Poor and Working? An Analysis of the Spending Patterns and Living Conditions of Working Poor Families in Canada." *Policy Research Initiative Research Papers Series.* Ottawa: Human Resources and Social Development Canada. Available online.

Forisha, B.L. 1978. *Sex Roles and Personal Awareness.* New Jersey: General Learning Press. Available online.

Freedman, Jonathan L. 1975. *Crowding and Behavior.* San Francisco: Freeman.

Freiler, Christa, Laurel Rothman, and Pedro Barata. May 2004. *Pathways to Progress: Structural Solutions to Address Child Poverty.* Toronto: Campaign2000.

Frideres, J.S. 1974. *Canada's Indians.* Scarborough, Ontario: Prentice-Hall.

Gee, Ellen, and Meredith M. Kimball. 1987. *Women and Aging.* Toronto: Butterworths.

Ghosh, Jayanti. 2010. "Poverty Reduction in China and India: Policy Implications of Recent Trends." DESA Working Paper No. 92. New York: United Nations, Department of Economic and Social Affairs. Available online.

Goffman, Nathan. 1963a. *Behavior in Public Places.* New York: The Free Press.

———. 1963b. *Stigma: Notes on the Management of Spoiled Identity.* Englewood Cliffs, NJ: Prentice Hall.

Goodman, Paul. 1956. *Growing Up Absurd.* New York: Random House.

Gordon, Milton M. 1964. *Assimilation in American Life.* New York: Oxford University Press.

Green, A.G. 1971. *Regional Aspects of Canada's Economic Growth.* Toronto: University of Toronto Press.

Greenberg, Michael, and David Green. 1999. *Raising the Floor: The Social and Economic Benefits of Minimum Wages in Canada.* Ottawa: Canadian Centre for Policy Alternatives.

Hannan, M.T., N.B. Tuma, and L.P. Groeneveld. 1977. "Income and Marital Events: Evidence from an Income-Maintenance Experience." *American Journal of Sociology* 82: 1186–1211.

Harding, Jim. 1971[1965]. "Canada's Indians: A Powerless Minority." In *Poverty in Canada,* edited by John Harp and John R. Hofley,239–252. Scarborough, Ontario: Prentice-Hall. First published by SUPA Research, Information and Publications Project, Canada.

Heilbroner, Robert L. 1980. *The Worldly Philosophers.* 5th ed. New York: Simon and Schuster.

Henry, Frances, and Effie Ginzberg. 1984. *Who Gets the Work: A Test of Racial Discrimination in Toronto.* Toronto: Urban Alliance on Race Relations.

Hewlett, Sylvia Ann. 1986. *A Lesser Life.* New York: William Marrow and Company Inc.

History of Canada Online. 2011. First Nations: Self Government. Available online.

Hoffer, Abram. 1962. *Niacin Therapy in Psychiatry.* Springfield, IL: Thomas Editions.

Homeless People—Rebecca's Story. 2008. Homeless.org. Available online.

Hudson, Christopher G. 2005. "Socioeconomic Status and Mental Illness: Tests of the Social Causation and Selection Hypotheses." *American Journal of Orthopsychiatry* 75 (1) (January): 3–18.

Human Resources and Skills Development Canada. n.d. "Hourly Minimum Wages in Canada for Adult Workers." *Labour.* Ottawa: Human Resources and Skills Development Canada. Last modified 2 March 2012. Available online.

Hundermark, Susan. 1985. "Rural Feminism." *Healthsharing* (Winter): 14–17.

Jackson, Andrew. 2004. "Gender Inequality and Precarious Work: Exploring the Impact of Unions through the Gender and Work Database'." Research Paper No. 31 for Gender and Work: Knowledge Production in Practice Conference. York University. Toronto, September 30 to October 2.

Jackson, J.A. 1970. *Sociological Studies 2: Migration.* Cambridge: Cambridge University Press.

Jaffe, Frederick, and Steven Polgar. 1968. "Family Planning and Public Policy: Is the 'Culture of Poverty' the New Cop-out?" *Journal of Marriage and Family* 30: 228–35.

Jarjoura, G.R., R.A. Triplett, and G. P. Brinkler. 2002. "Growing Up Poor: Examining the Link between Persistent Child Poverty and Delinquency." *Journal of Quantitative Criminology* 18: 159–187.

Johanson-Sirleaf, Ellen. Quoted in Roche, Douglas. 1976. *Charity Not Justice: The New Global Ethic for Canada,* 44–45. Toronto: McClelland and Stewart.

Jordan, B. 1996. *A Theory of Poverty and Social Exclusion.* Oxford: Polity Press.

JRank. 2008. *Consequences of Poverty, Poor Families Effects.* Available online.

Kazemipur, Abdolmohammad, and Shivalingappa S. Halli. 2000. *The New Poverty in Canada: Ethnic Groups and Ghetto Neighbourhoods.* Toronto: Thompson Educational.

Kelly, John G. 1988. *Pay Equity Management.* Don Mills: CCH Canadian Limited.

Kelly, K. 1995. "Visible Minorities: A Diverse Group." *Canadian Social Trends* 37: 2–8.

Klinenberg, E. 2002. *Heatwave: A Social Autopsy of Disaster in Chicago.* Chicago: University of Chicago Press.

Kneissl, Karin. 2011. "Elements for a Scientific Analysis of the Arab Revolutions in Spring 2011." *AAS Working Papers in Social Anthropology* 21: 1–17. Available online.

Kuhan, Randall. 2011. "On the Role of Human Development in the Arab Spring." Working paper. Josef Korbel School of International Studies, University of Denver, September.

Lambo, T. Adeoye. 2000. "Constraints on World Medical and Health Progress." In *One World: The Health and Survival of the Human Species in the 21st Century*, edited by Robert Lanza, 111–128. Santa Fe, NM: Health Press.

Law, Marc T., and Frazil Mihlar. 1998. *Is There a Youth Unemployment Crisis?* Fraser Institute Public Policy Sources, Number 14. Vancouver: The Fraser Institute. Available online.

Lee, Kevin. 2000. *Urban Poverty in Canada: A Statistical Profile.* Ottawa: CCSD. Available online.

Lewis, Oscar. 1966. *La Vida.* New York: Random House.

Lipman, E.L., D.R. Offord, and M.D. Dooley. 1996. "What Do We Know About Children from Single Mother Families?" In *Growing Up in Canada: National Longitudinal Survey of Children and Youth*, 83–91. Ottawa: Human Resources Department.

Lithwick, N.H. 1978. *Regional Economic Policy: The Canadian Experience.* Toronto: McGraw-Hill Ryerson.

Lochhead, C. 2003. *The Transition Penalty: Unemployment among Recent Immigrants to Canada.* Ottawa: Canadian Labour and Business Centre.

Loppie-Reading, Charlotte, and Fred Wien. 2009. *Health Inequalities and Social Determinants of Aboriginal Peoples' Health.* Ottawa: National Collaborating Centre for Aboriginal Health Centre for Aboriginal Health.

Lum, Thomas. 2006. *Social Unrest in China.* CRS Report for Congress, Congressional Research Services. Washington: Library of Congress. Available online.

MacLeod, Linda. 1987. *Battered but Not Beaten: Preventing Wife Battering in Canada.* Ottawa: Canadian Advisory Council on Status of Women.

Maddison, Angus. 2008. *Historical Statistics of World Economy 1-2008 AD.* Available online.

Malthus, Thomas R. 1826. *First Essay on Population.* London: J. Johnson.

Mansell, Robert L., and Lawrence Copithorne. 1986. "Canadian Regional Disparities: A Survey." In *Disparities and Interregional Adjustment* edited by Kenneth Norrie, 1–51. Toronto: University of Toronto Press.

Mayer, A.W. 1978. "The Influence of Family Income on Food Consumption Patterns and Nutrient Intake in Canada." *Canadian Journal of Public Health* (69): 208–21.

McDonald, Lynn. 2007. *Aging in Place.* Toronto: The Institute for Life Course and Aging, University of Toronto, 2007.

McInnis, M. 1968. "The Trend of Interregional Income Differentials in Canada." *Canadian Journal of Economics* 1: 440–470.

McIsaac, E. 2003. *Immigrants in Canadian Cities: Census 2001—What Do the Data Tell?* Ottawa: Policy Options.

McWhirter, W.R., H. Smith, and K.M. McWhirter. 1983. "Social Class as a Prognostic Variable in Acute Lymphoblastic Leukaemia." *Medical Journal of Australia* 2: 319–321.

Mead, George Herbert. 1934. *Mind, Self, and Society: From the Standpoint of a Social Behaviorist.* Ed. Charles W. Morris. Chicago: University of Chicago Press.

Mérette, Marcel. 2005. "Ageing, Retirement and Pensions." Paper presented at Perspective on Canada Conference organized by Statistics Canada Central Region. Toronto, 14 April.

Merton, Robert K. 1938. "Social Structure and Anomie." *American Sociological Review* 3: 672–82.

Mignone, J. 2003. *Measuring Social Capital: A Guide for First Nations Communities*. Ottawa: Canadian Institute for Health Information.

———, and J. O'Neil. 2005. "Social Capital and Youth Suicide Risk Factors in First Nations Communities." *Canadian Journal of Public Health* 96(Suppl 1): S51–54.

Miller, Walter B. 1958. "Lower Class Culture as a Generating Milieu of Gang Delinquency." *Journal of Social Issues* 15: 15–19.

Miron, John, R. 1988. *Housing in Postwar Canada: Demographic Change, Housing Formation and Housing Demand*. Montreal: McGill-Queen's University Press.

Mock, Karen. 1986. *Child Care Needs of Cultural Minorities*. Report prepared for the Special Committee on Child Care. Ottawa: Queen's Printer.

Morissette, René, and Xuelin Zhang. 2004. "Retirement plan awareness." *Persepctives*. Statistics Canada Catalogue no. 75-001-XIE. Ottawa: Statistics Canada.

Morris, Marika. 2002. "What It Is Like to be Poor." In *Women and Poverty*, 3rd ed. Ottawa: Canadian Research Institute for the Advancement of Women. Available online.

Munro, J.M. 1978. "Regional Economic Policies in Canada." *Canadian Journal of Regional Science* 11: 61–76.

Murray, Stuart, and Hugh Mackenzie. 2007. *Bringing Minimum Wage Above the Poverty Line*. Ottawa: Canadian Centre for Policy Alternatives.

Myles, J. 2012. "Social Composition of the Elderly." In *Aging. The Canadian Encyclopedia*. Available online.

National Council of Welfare. 1975. *Poor Kids*. Ottawa: National Council of Welfare.

———. 1979. *Women and Poverty*. Ottawa: National Council of Welfare.

———. 1981. *The Working Poor: The People and Programs*. Ottawa: National Council of Welfare.

———. February 1984. *Sixty-five and Older*. Ottawa: National Council of Welfare.

———. April 1984. *A Pension Primer*. Ottawa: National Council of Welfare.

———.1987. *1987 Poverty Lines*. Ottawa: National Council of Welfare.

———. April 1988. *Poverty Profile 1988*. Ottawa: National Council of Welfare.

———. 1988. *Child Care*. Ottawa: National Council of Welfare.

———. 1989. *A Pension Primer*. Ottawa: National Council of Welfare.

———.1990. *Women and Poverty Revisited*. Ottawa: National Council of Welfare.

———. 1998. *Poverty Profile 1998*. Ottawa: National Council of Welfare.

———. 2004. *Poverty Profile 2001*. Ottawa: National Council of Welfare.

———. 2005. *Welfare Incomes 2004*. Ottawa: National Council of Welfare.

———. 2007. *First Nations, Métis and Inuit Children Youth: Time to Act*. Ottawa: National Council of Welfare.

———. March 2007. "Poverty among Seniors by Province." *Poverty Statistics 2004*. Ottawa: National Council of Welfare.

———. 2008. *Poverty Profile 2002 and 2003*. Ottawa: National Council of Welfare.

———. 2012. *Child Welfare Income 2009*. Ottawa: National Council of Welfare. Available online.

National Seniors Council. 2009. *Report of the National Seniors Council on Low Income among Seniors*. Ottawa: National Seniors Council. Available online.

Newfoundland & Labrador Statistics Agency, Statistics Canada/Economics and Statistics Branch. 2009. *Labour Force Survey*. Available online.

Offord, David R., Michael H. Boyle, and Beverly R. Jones. 1987. "Psychiatric Disorder and Poor School Performance among Welfare Children in Ontario." *Canadian Journal of Psychiatry* 32 (October).

Ontario Ministry of Culture and Recreation. 1982. *Mother Tongue Atlas*. Toronto: Ontario Ministry of Culture and Recreation.

Organisation for Economic Co-operation and Development (OECD), Directorate for Employment, Labour and Social Affairs. 2008. *Growing Unequal? Income Distribution and Poverty in OECD Countries.* Paris: OECD. Available online.

OECD. 2011. *Special Focus: Inequality in Emerging Economies (EES).* Paris: OECD. Available online.

Ornstein, Michael D., and Raghubar D. Sharma. 1983. *Adjustment and Economic Experience of Immigrants in Canada: 1976 Longitudinal Survey of Immigrants.* Toronto: Institute for Behavioural Research, York University.

Pal, Parthapratim, and Jayanti Ghosh. 2007. "Inequality in India a Survey of Recent Trends." DESA Working Paper No. 45. New York: United Nations, Department of Economic and Social Affairs. Available online.

Park, Robert E., and Ernest W. Burgess. 1925. *The City.* Chicago: University of Chicago Press.

Park, Robert R. 1950. *Race and Culture.* Glencoe: The Free Press.

Paugam, S., ed. 1996. *L'exclusion: L'état des Savoirs.* Paris: La Découverte.

Peace, Robin. 2001. "Social Exclusion: A Concept in Need of Definition?" *Social Policy Journal of New Zealand* 16: 17–35. Available online.

Pike, Robert. 1975. "Legal Access and the Incidence of Divorce in Canada: A Sociological Analysis." *Canadian Review of Sociology and Anthropology* 12.

Porter, John. 1965. *The Vertical Mosaic.* Toronto: University of Toronto Press. Quoted in Anthony Richmond and Ravi P. Verma. 1978. "Income Inequality in Canada: Ethnic and Generational Aspect." *Canadian Studies in Population* 5: 26.

Porter, John, Marion Porter, and Bernard Blishen. 1982. *Stations and Callings: Making it Through Ontario's Schools.* Toronto: Methuen.

Ram, Bali. August 1986. "Women's Labour Force Participation and Child Care in Canada: Socio-Demographic Aspects." XIth World Congress of Sociology. New Delhi.

———. October 1987. "Family Structure and Extramarital Child Care Need in Canada: Some Projections." *Contributions to Demography: Methodology and Substantive.* Edmonton: University of Alberta, Department of Sociology.

———, and Feng Hou. 2003. "Change in Family Structure and Child Outcomes: Role of Economic and Familial Resources." *The Policy Studies Journal* 31(3).

Reitz, Jeffrey. 2005. *Tapping Immigrants' Skills: New Directions for Canadian Immigration Policy in the Knowledge Economy.* Montreal: Institute for Research on Public Policy.

Richmond, Anthony H. 1979. "Ethnic Segregation of Immigrants in Toronto." *Canadian Review of Sociology and Anthropology* 16: 228–230.

———. 1988. *Immigration and Ethnic Conflict.* London: Macmillan.

Richmond, Anthony, and Ravi P. Verma. 1978. "Income Inequality in Canada: Ethnic and Generational Aspect." *Canadian Studies in Population* 5: 25–36.

Roach, J.L., and O.R. Gursslin. 1967. "An Evaluation of the Concept of 'Culture of Poverty.'" *Social Forces* 45(3): 383–392.

Robertson, Ian. 1977. *Sociology.* New York: Worth Publishers Inc.

Roche, Douglas. 1976. *Justice Not Charity: A New Global Ethic for Canada.* Toronto: McClelland and Stewart.

Rodgers, G., C. Gore, and J. Figueiredo, eds. 1995. *Social Exclusion: Rhetoric, Reality, Responses.* Geneva: International Labour Office.

Room, G., ed. 1995. *Beyond the Threshold: The Measurement and Analysis of Social Exclusion.* Bristol, UK: The Policy Press.

Rotz, Dana. 2004. *Why Have Divorce Rates Fallen? The Role of Women's Age at Marriage.* Boston: Harvard University. Available online.

Russell, S.J. 1978. *Sex Role Socialization in High School: A Study in Perpetuation of Patriarchal Culture.* Ph.D. Thesis. Toronto: University of Toronto, Department of Sociology.

Russell, Susan. 1987. "The Hidden Curriculum of School: Reproducing Gender and Class Hierarchies." In *Feminism and Political Economy*, edited by Heather Jon Maroney and Meg Luxton, 197–212. Toronto: Methuen.

Salsberg Ezrin, Sharyn A. 1989. "The Balancing Act: Women Are the Key to Making It Work." *The Toronto Star,* 4 May. L1.

Sandefur, Garry D., and Wilber J. Scott. 1983. "Minority Group Status and the Wages of Indian and Black Males." *Social Science Research* 12: 44–68.

Sarlo, Chris. 2000. *The Wage and Poverty: A Critical Evaluation.* A Report for the Canadian Restaurant and Foodservices Association, Halifax: CRFSA. Available online.

Saskatchewan Department of Social Services. 1974. *Client Housing: A Survey of the Housing Conditions of Saskatchewan Assistance Plan Recipients: Adequacy, Rent and Ownership, Regina.*

Satzewich, Vic. 2011. *Racism in Canada.* Don Mills, Ontario: Oxford University Press.

Sen, Amartya. 2000. *Social Exclusion: Concept, Application, and Scrutiny.* Manila, Philippines: Asian Development Bank.

Shah, Chandrakant P., Meldon Kahan, and John Krauser. 1987. "The Health of Children of Low-Income Families." *Canadian Medical Association Journal* 137 (15 September): 485–490.

Shannon, Michael T., and Charles M. Beach. 1995. "Distributional Employment Effects of Ontario Minimum Wage Proposals: A Microdata Approach." *Canadian Public Policy* 21(3): 284–303.

Sharma, Raghubar D. 1980a. *Migration and Fertility in a Western Canadian Metropolis.* Ph.D. (Sociology) thesis. Edmonton: University of Alberta.

———. 1980b. *Immigrant Needs in Metropolitan Toronto.* Toronto: Institute for Behavioural Research, York University.

———. 1981a. *Perceived Difficulties of Foreign-born Population and Services of Agencies.* Toronto: Institute for Behavioural Research, York University.

———. 1981b. *A Multivariate Analysis of Difficulties Reported by Long Term Third World and Non-Anglophone Immigrants, in Toronto Three Years or More.* Toronto: Institute for Behavioural Research, York University.

———. 1982a. "Pre-marital and Ex-nuptial Fertility (Illegitimacy) in Canada 1921-1972." *Canadian Studies in Population* 9: 1–15.

———. 1982b. *Trends in Demographic and Socio-economic Characteristics of Metropolitan Toronto Population.* Toronto: Institute for Behavioural Research, York University.

———. 1987. 'First Marriage Decrement Tables, Ontario, Males and Females 1971, 1976, and 1981." *Genus* 43 (3–4): 61–68.

Singer, J.D. 1987. Quoted in Shah, Chandrakant P., Meldon Kahan, and John Krauser. "The Health of Children of Low-income Families." *Canadian Medical Association Journal* (137): 485–90.

Smith, Ekuwa, and Andrew Jackson. 2002. *Does a Rising Tide Lift All Boats? The Labour Market Experiences and Incomes of Recent Immigrants 1995 to 1998.* Ottawa: Canadian Council on Social Development.

Social Assistance Review Committee. 1988. *TRANSITIONS.* Prepared for the Ontario Ministry of Community and Social Services. Toronto: Queen's Printers.

Social Planning Council of Kitchener-Waterloo. 2000. Available online.

Social Planning Council of Metropolitan Toronto. 1983. *Social Infopac* 3(2).

Spears, John. 1989. "Family Battles Poverty in Rural New Brunswick." *The Toronto Star,* 27 February. A18.

Speirs, Rosemary. 1989. "Natives' plight a national tragedy." *Canada's Native Population.* Statistics Canada Catalogue no. 99-937. Ottawa: Information Canada.

Spencer, Herbert. 1961. *The Study of Sociology.* Ann Arbor: University of Michigan.

Sprankle, Judith K. 1986. *Working It Out.* New York: Walker and Company.

St-Arnaud, Julie, Marie P. Beaudet, and Patricia Tully. 2005. "Life Expectancy." *Health Reports* 17(1). Statistics Canada Catalogue no. 82-003. Ottawa: Statistics Canada. Available online.

Statistics Canada, Demography Division. 2008. *Canadian Demographics at a Glance.* Available online.

———, Income Statistics Division. 2010. *Low Income Lines 2008–09.* Statistics Canada Catalogue no. 75F002M–No. 005. Ottawa: Statistics Canada. Available online.

———. n.d. Average Hourly Wages of Employees by Selected Characteristics and Profession, Unadjusted Data, by Province (Monthly). Available online.

———. 1984. *Canada's Lone Parent Families.* Statistics Canada Catalogue no. 99-933. Ottawa: Minister of Supply and Services.

———. 1996. "Table 1: Visible Minorities in Canada." *Statistics Profile Series.* Statistics Canada Catalogue no. 85F0033MIE. Ottawa: Canadian Centre for Justice.

———. 1998. *Low Income Measures, Low Income After Tax Cut-Offs and Low Income After Tax Measure.* Statistics Canada Catalogue no. 13F0019XIB. Ottawa: Statistics Canada.

———. 1999. *Low Income Cut-Offs (LICOs).* Statistics Canada Catalogue no. 13-551-XPB. Ottawa: Statistics Canada.

———. 16 July 2002. "Profile of the Canadian Population by Age and Sex: Canada Ages." *Analytical Series.* Ottawa: Statistics Canada.

———. October 2002. *Profile of Canadian Families and Households, Diversification Continues.* Statistics Canada Catalogue no. F0030XIE200103. Ottawa: Statistics Canada.

———. 2003a. *Census 2001.* Statistics Canada Catalogue no. 97F0011XVB01046. Ottawa: Minister of Industry.

———. 2003b. *Participation and Activity Limitation Survey, 2001—Children with Disabilities and Their Families.* Ottawa: Statistics Canada.

———. 2004a. "More Seniors Living with a Spouse, More Living Alone and Fewer Living in Health Care Institutions." *Analytical Series, 2001 Census.* Ottawa: Statistics Canada.

———. 2004b. *Income Trends in Canada 2004.* Statistics Canada Catalogue no. 75-202-XIE. Ottawa: Statistics Canada. Cited in "Economic Security Fact Sheet #2: Poverty." *Stats and Facts.* Canadian Council on Social Development. Available online.

———. 23 July 2004. "Study: Housing Costs of Elderly Families." *The Daily.* Ottawa: Statistics Canada.

———. 2005. "Table 11.1." *Income in Canada 2005.* Statistics Canada Catalogue no.75-202-XIE. Ottawa: Statistics Canada.

———. 1 February 2005. "Health Indicators." *The Daily.* Ottawa: Statistics Canada.

———. 3 February 2005. "Decline in Homeownership Rates among Immigrant Families." *The Daily.* Ottawa: Statistics Canada.

———. June 2005. *Canadian Price Index Tables.* Ottawa: Statistics Canada.

———. 2006a. "Chapter 6: Aboriginal Seniors in Canada." *A Portrait of Seniors in Canada.* Statistics Canada Catalogue no. 89-519-XWE. Ottawa: Statistics Canada. Available online.

———. 2006b. *Women in Canada.* 5th ed. Ottawa: Statistics Canada.

———. 6 June 2006. *Aboriginal People as Victims and Offenders 2004.* Ottawa: Information Canada.

———. 2007a. *2006 Census.* Statistics Canada Catalogue no. 97-554-XCB2006007. Ottawa: Statistics Canada. Available online.

———. 2007b. *A Portrait of Seniors in Canada, 2006.* Statistics Canada Catalogue no. 89-579XIE. Ottawa: Statistics Canada. Available online.

————.9 May 2007 (modified). "Table 1." *Per Capita Personal Disposable Income.* Available online.

————. 2008. "Unemployment Rates by Age." *Canadian Market at a Glance.* Statistics Canada Catalogue no. 71-222-X. Ottawa: Statistics Canada.

————. January 2008. "Aboriginal People in Canada in 2006: Inuit, Métis and First Nations, 2006." Statistics Canada Catalogue no. 97-558-XIE. Ottawa: Information Canada.

————. 5 May 2008 (modified). "Table 11.1." *Income in Canada 2005.* Statistics Canada Catalogue no. 75-202-XIE. Ottawa: Statistics Canada. Available online.

————. 21 November 2008 (modified). "Census Snap Shot." *Canadian Social Trends.* Statistics Canada Catalogue no. 11-008 XWE. Ottawa: Statistics Canada. Available online.

————. 3 June 2009 (modified). "Table 1-1." *Income in Canada.* Statistics Canada Catalogue no. 75-202-X. Ottawa: Statistics Canada.

————. 22 July 2009. "Study: Guaranteed Income Supplement Update." *The Daily.* Ottawa: Statistics Canada.

————. 2010. "Tables 202-0802 and 202-0804." *Income in Canada.* Statistics Canada Catalogue no. 75-202-X. Ottawa: Statistics Canada.

————. June 2010. *Population Projections for Canada, Provinces and Territories, 2009 to 2036.* Statistics Canada Catalogue no. 91-520-X. Ottawa: Statistics Canada.

————. 17 September 2010. *Child and Spousal Support: Maintenance Enforcement Survey Statistics.* Ottawa: Statistics Canada. Available online.

————. June 2011a. "CANSIM Table 202-0802." *Persons in Low Income After Tax.* Statistics Canada Catalogue no. 75-202-X. Ottawa: Statistics Canada.

————. June 2011b. "Table H: Income Social Indicators." *Canadian Social Trends.* Statistics Canada Catalogue no. 11-008-X. Ottawa: Statistics Canada. Available online.

————. 22 August 2011. "Total Fertility Rate 1926 to 2008." Ottawa: Statistics Canada. Available online.

————. 6 January 2012 (modified). "CANSIM Table 282-0002." *Labour Force, Employed and Unemployed, Numbers and Rates, by Province.* Available online.

————.20 January 2012 (modified). "CANSIM Table 326-0021" and Statistics Canada Catalogue nos. 62-001-X and 62-010-X. Ottawa: Statistics Canada.

————. 24 February 2012 (modified). *Women in Canada: A Gender-based Statistical Report.* Statistics Canada Catalogue no. 89-503-X. Ottawa: Statistics Canada. Available online.

Stefaniuk, Walter. 1989. "Giving Poor Kids a Boost." *The Toronto Star,* 24 January. D1.

Stewart, V. 1976. "Social Influences on Sex Differences in Behaviour." In *Sex Differences,* edited by M. S. Teitelbaum, 156–157. New York: Doubleday.

Stone, Leroy O., and Michael J. MacLean. 1979. *Future Income Prospects for Canada's Senior Citizens.* Toronto: Butterworths.

Sun, Liping. 2011. Quoted in "Protests and Demonstrations in China: The Tensions and Methods Behind Them." factsanddetails.com. Available online.

Sussman, Debra, and Martin Tabi. March 2004. "Minimum Wage Workers." *Perspectives.* Statistics Canada Catalogue no. 75-001-XIE. Ottawa: Statistics Canada. Available online.

Sutherland, Edwin H. 1949. *White Collar Crime.* New York: Holt, Rinehart and Winston.

Teotonio, Isabel. 2011. "Patricia Cummings-Diaz: Society Reflects that I'm a Failure." *The Toronto Star,* 4 June.

Torjman, Sherri. 1987. *The Reality Gap.* Ottawa: Canadian Advisory Council on the Status of Women.

Toronto Star, The. 7 December 1990. "Mandatory Retirement Upheld." A1.

Transitions. 1988. Report of the Social Assistance Review Committee. Toronto: Queen's Printers.

United Nations Children's Fund (UNICEF). 2005. *The State of the World's Children 2005.* New York: The United Nations Children's Fund.

United Nations Development Programme (UNDP). 2005. *Human Development Report.* New York: UNDP.

———. 2011. *Human Development Report.* New York: UNDP.

United Nations. 2009. *The Millennium Development Goals Report.* New York: United Nations. Available online.

United States of America. Congressional Budget Office (CBO). 2011. *Trends in the Distribution of Household Income between 1979 and 2007.* Washington: Congress of the United States.

Vásquez, Ian. 2001. "Ending Mass Poverty." Washington: CATO Institute. Available online.

———. 2002. "Globalization and the Poor." *The Independent Review* 7 (2): 197–206.

Veerle, Miranda. 2011. *Cooking, Caring and Volunteering: Unpaid Work around the World.* Paris: Organisation for Economic Co-operation and Development. Available online.

Vranken, Jan. 1996. No Social Cohesion without Social Exclusion? Eurex Lecture 4. *OASeS.* Antwerp: University of Antwerpen. Available online.

Waite, L.J., and Moore, A.K. 1978. "The Impact of an Early First Birth on Young Women's Educational Attainment." *Social Forces* 56: 845–865.

Walker, J., and C. Herbitter. 2005. *Aging in the Shadows: Social Isolation among Seniors in New York City.* New York: United Neighborhood House.

Ward, Karen. 4 January 2011. *The World in 2050: Quantifying the Shift in Global Economy.* HSBC Global Research. Available online.

Waxman, Chaim I. 1977. *Stigma of Poverty.* New York: Pergamon Press.

Weaver, Clyde, and Thomas Gunton. 1982. "From Drought Assistance to Mega Projects: Fifty Years of Regional Theory and Policy in Canada." *Canadian Journal of Regional Science* 5: 5–37.

Wedderburn, Dorothy. 1970. "A Cross-National Study of Standards of Living of the Aged in Three Countries." In *The Concept of Poverty,* edited by Peter Townsend, 193–204. London: Heinemann.

Wedge, Peter, and Hilary Prosser. 1973. *Born to Fail?* London: Arrow Books Ltd.

Whyte, Donald A. 1965. "Sociological Aspects of Poverty: A Conceptual Analysis." *The Canadian 150 Review of Sociology and Anthropology* 2:4.

Wolfson, Michael, and John Evans. 1989. *Statistics Canada's Low Income Cut-offs Methodological Concerns and Possibilities: A Discussion Paper.* Ottawa: Statistics Canada.

World Health Organization (WHO). 2011. *World Health Statistics, 2011, Global Health Indicators, Part II, Table 7.* Geneva: WHO. Available online.

Yalnizyan, Armine. 2000. *Canada's Greatest Divide.* Toronto: The Centre for Justice Foundation for Research and Education.

Yinger, J. Milton. 1960. "Contraculture and Subculture." *American Sociological Review* 25: 625–35.

Index